Cast of Mind

B. Ingrid Olson

[RE: CAST OF MIND] INTRO-RETROSPECTION

B. Ingrid Olson

I received an invitation to create a yearlong exhibition at i8 Grandi in Reykjavík, Iceland, in 2023. Now, the project continues in this book.

Mood Order

The title *Cast of Mind* comes from a metaphorical phrase describing the way that a person might perceive something due to a certain disposition or ingrained belief system, or perhaps as the consequence of a more passing feeling or outlook. Tragedy, love, hunger—all affective lenses, or states of being, through which to see and understand the world from a specific oblique. While the expression encapsulates the idea of subjective, temperamental modes of perception, its component words can also be pulled apart to poetically suggest making a permanent record of the act of thinking. A physical imprint. A cast of one's mind. The attempt to form a hard copy out of something as slippery as a thought process is an appropriate frame for this exhibition, which was understood from the outset to be subject to change.

How are cognition, decision-making, memory, or instinct evidenced?

I have approached the exhibition as a network of associations, a thought map, that expands and collapses throughout the year. The gallery becomes a site of both production and display, as newly completed works arrive from my studio at regular intervals to be situated with older, extant works. Every four weeks or so, the artworks are shifted and architectural features are adjusted. Each work adds a seed, arterial spread, neural bomb, webbed to the other works around it. Sometimes subtracting a work: A light is turned out, an afterimage appears, a silhouette outlines an extraction. By the end of the year, there are ten distinct iterations of one exhibition, enumerated I to X in this book.

Introduction to Introductions: A Small Room

During my first visit to i8 Grandi, I perceive its two rooms as distinct yet connected spaces, like a proscenium and a stage. In the exhibition, the small gallery just inside the entryway serves as a calibration, or a primer, for an encounter just beyond. The works located in this interstitial space act as a preamble, setting the speed and tone by which to approach the installation in the larger adjacent room.

Table

Present for all ten iterations, *Total Work (Cast of Mind)*, 2023, is a structure akin to a worktable. Outsized for the room, the semifunctional form occupies the majority of the floor space and establishes a narrow perimeter between its edges and the surrounding walls that a visitor must negotiate. The table-cum-sculpture holds configurations of artworks and books that shift over time within a cycle of assembly and disassembly. At the beginning, unattached tabletop panels are stacked loosely on a base; they are then rearranged, still unattached; after that, they are affixed to the base panel by panel to form a single plane; and finally, they are again completely taken apart. The artworks displayed on top of the table are distinct, nameable, and (re)movable.

Walls

The walls of the small room support a four-part text work, six photographic works, and one wall-mounted relief—each tied to the activity and space required for thinking. Interiors, models, desks, drawings, blank pages, changeable subjectivity, unachievable objectivity, mistakes, and the cranial cavity itself. The text work, *Introductions by Kate*

Zambreno, 2018/2023, replicates a text by Kate Zambreno that served as an introduction to another, earlier exhibition and is re-sited in *Cast of Mind*. The black vinyl letters are applied on a wall built over an existing window, the invisible fenestration mapped out by the outer dimensions of the text block, like an X-ray penetrating the drywall.

Turn to Your Left

The second room of the gallery is spatially exaggerated, with a relatively long and narrow floor plan and a soaring ceiling. Throughout *Cast of Mind*, site-responsive gestures within this space accentuate and attenuate the dramatic proportions of the architecture: a nearly invisible mural; holes drilled into the walls; a group of low-hanging light fixtures in shifting formations; and temporary architectural structures, which are designed to condition and impede the experience of the space. The thinking in this large room is embodied, felt near the navel somewhere.

Constants

Throughout the run of the exhibition, the glossy off-white mural *Reflective Comedy, standing shoulder wall*, 2023, painted to my shoulder height, marks a bodily register within the outsized space. *What I would be if I wasn't what I am, I, I*, n.d., is a constellation of modified antique light fixtures that falls to a height just above the top edge of the wall painting. In their lengthy suspension, the ten fixtures create the illusion of a dropped ceiling bisecting the expansive gallery. Arranged variously throughout the year, the lights first span the entire space in an even grid, but then move incrementally closer together and back, forming a tight, spotlight-like cluster as they narrow in on the room's terminus.

Subtraction, Addition, Division, Multiplication

In each of the two rooms, a wall previously built in front of a window is pierced with a small circular hole. On four occasions, the apertures of *A small bore of light, but did it see her*, 2023, are enlarged to emit increasingly generous flashes of natural light. By the end of the summer, the windows are completely excavated. Just after, a short partial wall is built across the width of the large room. Constructed to my shoulder height, *Sluice (A weird rewriting of negative capability?)*, 2023, is fitted with a recessed metal aperture, or viewfinder. Behind the wall, replicas of the tabletop panels from *Total Work (Cast of Mind)* lie on the floor as an incomplete copy of their supported progenitors. Just as the original worktable has hosted various artworks on the flat plane of its topmost surface, *Total Work (Rest)*, 2023, serves as a small stage for the entire group of drawings, paintings, and ceramics that were included on the original table in previous iterations. By making this array of objects physically inaccessible—setting them behind the gated wall—the possibility of an in-the-round sculptural encounter is transformed into a flattened and fixed photographic relay.

"Pausing" Is Still a Gerund

For every subtraction or division, the inverse is also true. By taking a wall away, a window is revealed. By adding a wall, the space is doubled. The second guesses lead to new generations. The incidentals breed gestures. The incubation times are increased and some are still ongoing, failing to appear here (or there). This exhibition is a marathon of duration, encouraging a sense of continuum. Each pause is active. Elements, materials, and images are pushed and pulled, slipping in and out of situation. The ensemble of artworks on view is altered nearly monthly. Works change, not all at once but with each one moving in its own time. More closely related to a spiral than a line, the permutations of *Cast of Mind* do not reach culmination and instead tangle into a networked maze, composing an abstraction of both exhibition-making and studio processes. In January 2023, I wrote: An artistic practice is a living thing, not meant to be stabilized. Years later: An artistic practice is a living thing, not meant to be stabilized.

Iteration I

January 20–February 20, 2023

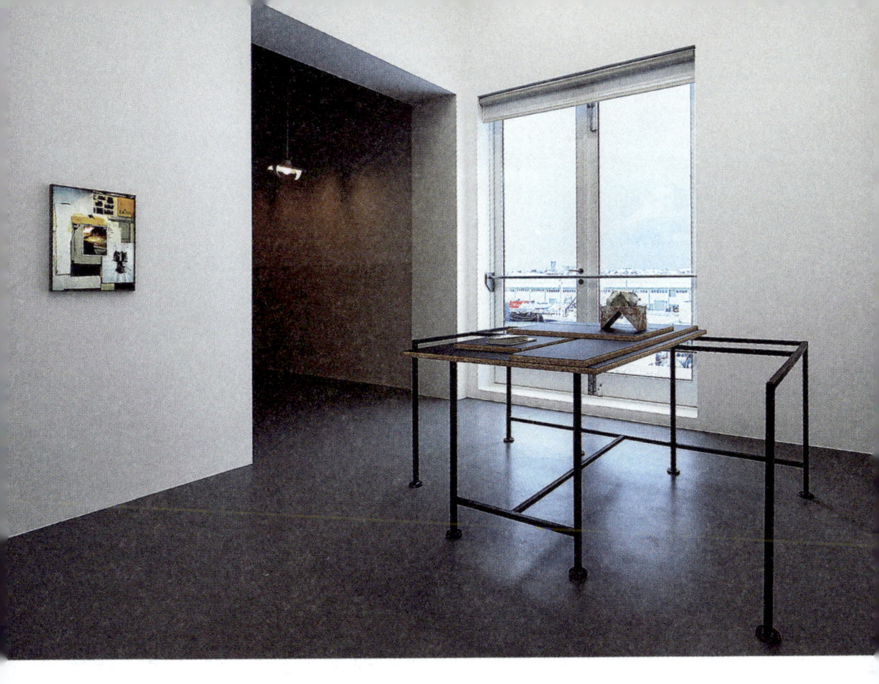

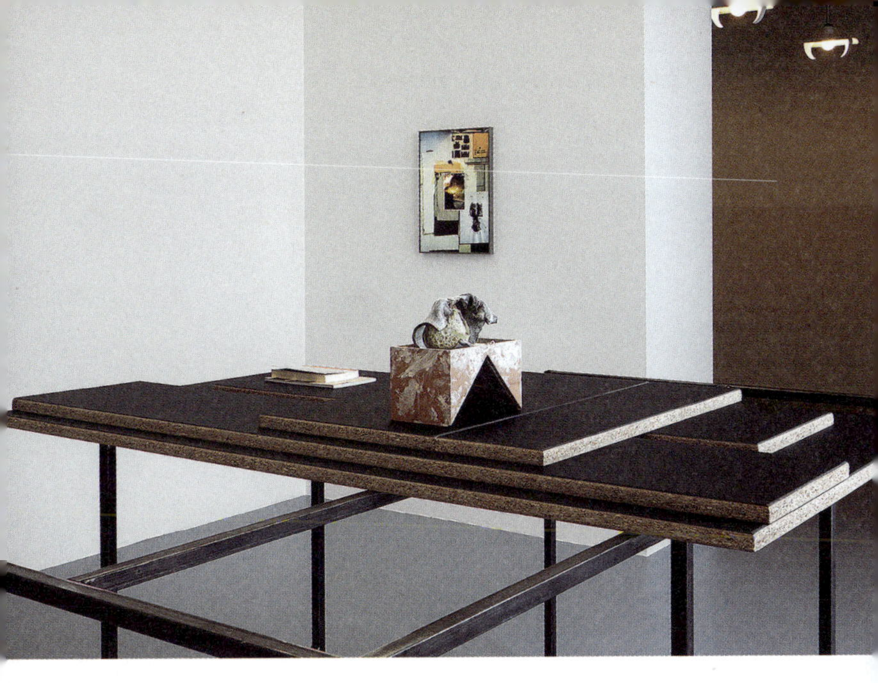

A Feminine Thought (1934–2021), 2021–22

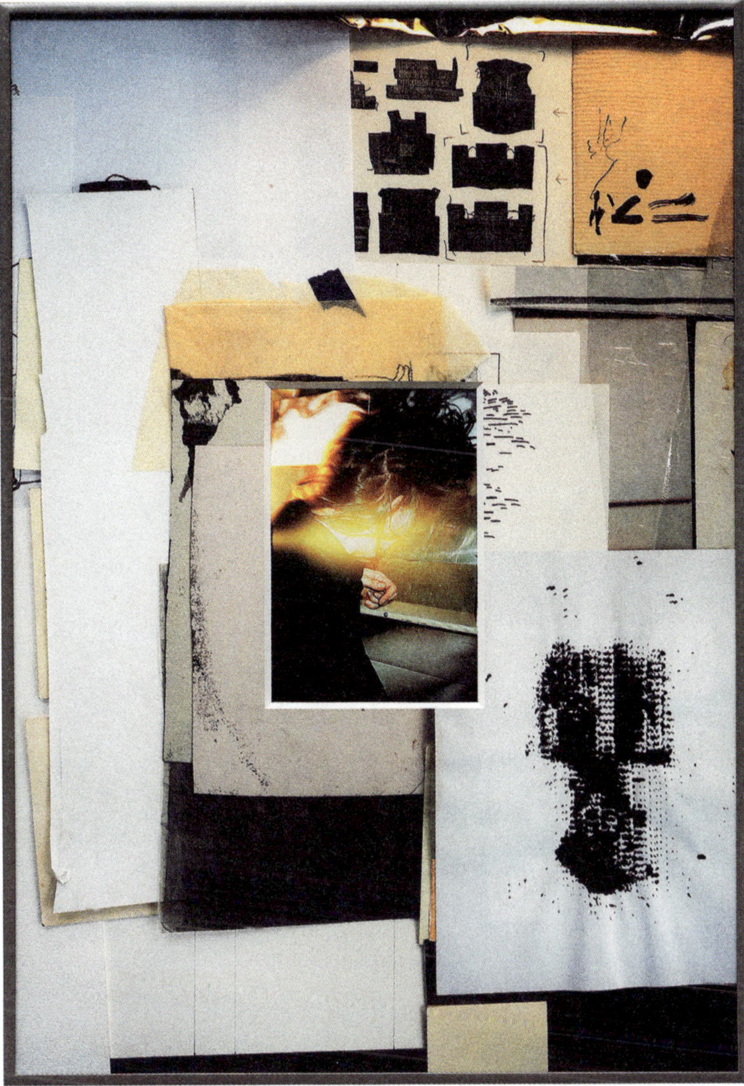

Feminine Thought, model, 2022–23

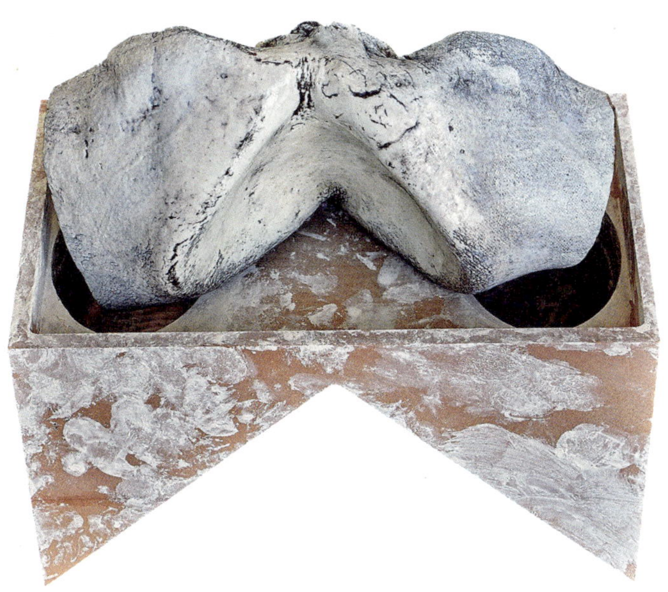

Total Work (Cast of Mind), 2023

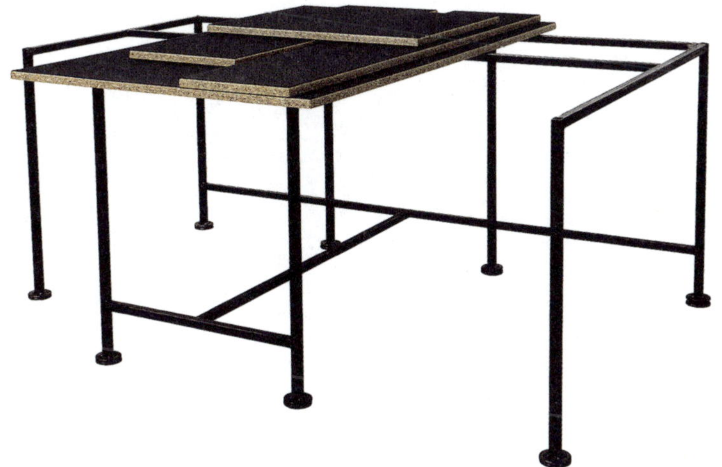

Introductions by Kate Zambreno (replica), 2018/2023

BODY PARSED, THREE ROOMS

To write an introduction is to double oneself. Is to fold one's thoughts into another. To fold one's body into another body. To fold one's text into another text. What is my body and what is your body. What is my text and what is your text. What is my space and what is your space. We have to remove our limbs in order to fit inside this book. How to write an introduction for a book that will be destroyed after certain period of time. Only those who are in the dark room can read it. Is this utopian, I wonder. I stay inside a dark room and write. Time has a different insistency now.

I read Elizabeth Grosz's *Architecture from the Outside*. I copy half of it down in my notebook, and then can't read my handwriting. From her introduction: "One cannot be outside everything, always outside: to be outside something is always to be inside something else." I like thinking about this but don't really know what this means. I write this out on a pad of paper; my hand hurts. I am in the room reading. I am on the couch. I type this out on my computer, and my laptop becomes part of my body. I am inside this book; I am inside this room; I am inside this body; I am outside this book; I am outside this room; I am outside this body. In my notebook I write this down again, to try to understand it: One cannot be outside everything, always outside: to be outside something is always to be inside something else.

I ask the man in the room with me what I should write about. I say, Do you remember when I spoke about this book, the one that had open windows or doors. Does it have open windows or doors or does it have no windows or doors. I say, Do you remember when I was inside of it, and I could not go outside of it, the book became my body, or was my body always a book. While waiting to write my notes on this book, I drink a green smoothie that he made for me. I name a future and imaginary child. I become the couch, scattered with books and notebooks. I look at boots online for my feet. I write three emails. I look at a photograph on my phone of a pregnant body. I google "Why does my baby have red cheeks"? I receive a package in the mail. I write this introduction while very full, and crouched over a pillow on the couch, and in another position, my legs in the air. I write this introduction while wearing leggings and an open robe, my breasts accessible. I write this introduction while wearing the same white set of overalls with coffee stains for four days. My body is a sentence. These gestures are ellipsis.

Time has passed. It's been years. I have been asked to add a note to the second edition. My feelings about the book remain the same.

BODY PARSED, THREE ROOMS

To write an introduction is to double oneself. Is to fold one's thoughts into another. To fold one's body into another body. To fold one's text into another text. What is my body and what is your body. What is my text and what is your text. What is my space and what is your space. We have to remove our limbs in order to fit inside this book. How to write an introduction for a book that will be destroyed after a certain period of time. Only those who are in the dark room can read it. Is this utopian, I wonder. I stay inside a dark room and write. Time has a different insistency now.

I read Elizabeth Grosz's *Architecture from the Outside*. I copy half of it down in my notebook, and then can't read my handwriting. From her introduction: "One cannot be outside everything, always outside: to be outside something is always to be inside something else." I like thinking about this but don't really know what this means. I write this out on a pad of paper; my hand hurts. I am in the room reading. I am on the couch. I type this out on my computer, and my laptop becomes part of my body. I am inside this book; I am inside this room; I am inside this body; I am outside this book; I am outside this room; I am outside this body. In my notebook I write this down again, to try to understand it: One cannot be outside everything, always outside: to be outside something is always to be inside something else.

I ask the man in the room with me what I should write about. I say, Do you remember when I spoke about this book, the one that had open windows and doors. Does it have open windows or doors or does it have no windows or doors. I say, Do you remember when I was inside of it, and I could not go outside of it, the book became my body, or was my body always a book. While waiting to write my notes on this book, I drink a green smoothie that he made for me. I name a future and imaginary child. I become the couch, scattered with books and notebooks. I look at boots online for my feet. I write three emails. I look at a photograph on my phone of a pregnant body. I google "Why does my baby have red cheeks"? I receive a package in the mail. I write this introduction while very full, and crouched over a pillow on the couch, and in another position, my legs in the air. I write this introduction while wearing leggings and an open robe, my breasts accessible. I write this introduction while wearing the same white set of overalls with coffee stains for four days. My body is a sentence. These gestures are ellipsis.

Time has passed. It's been years. I have been asked to add a note to the second edition. My feelings about the book remain the same.

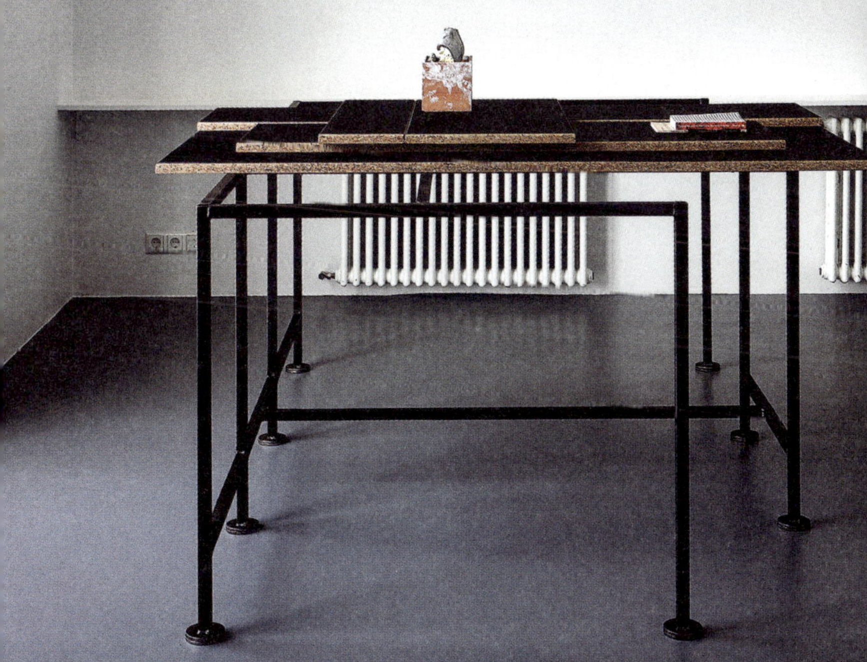

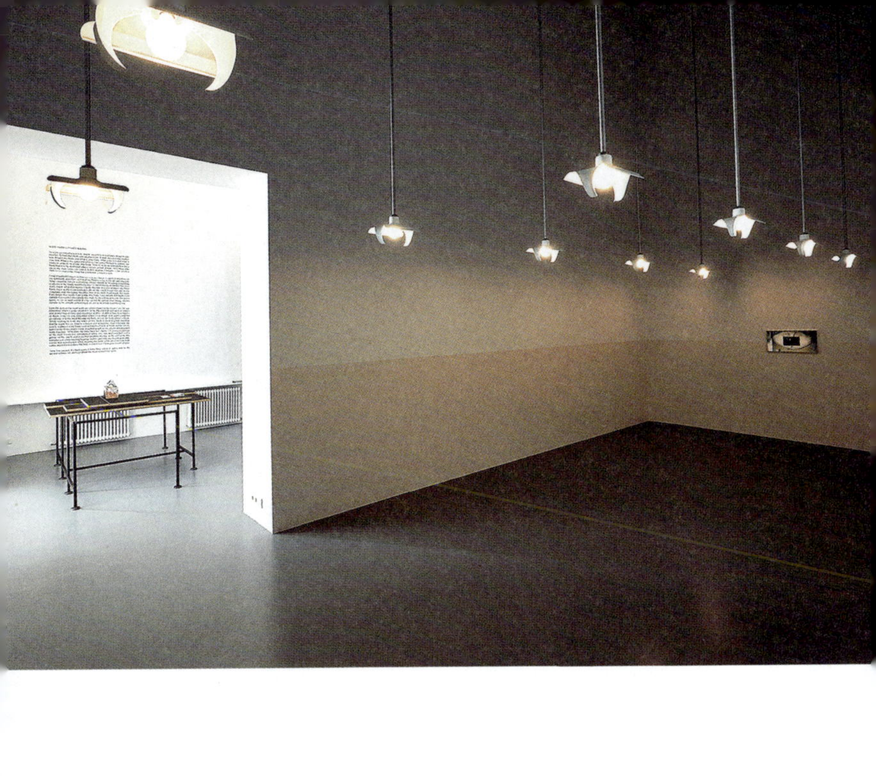

What I would be if I wasn't what I am, I, I, n.d.

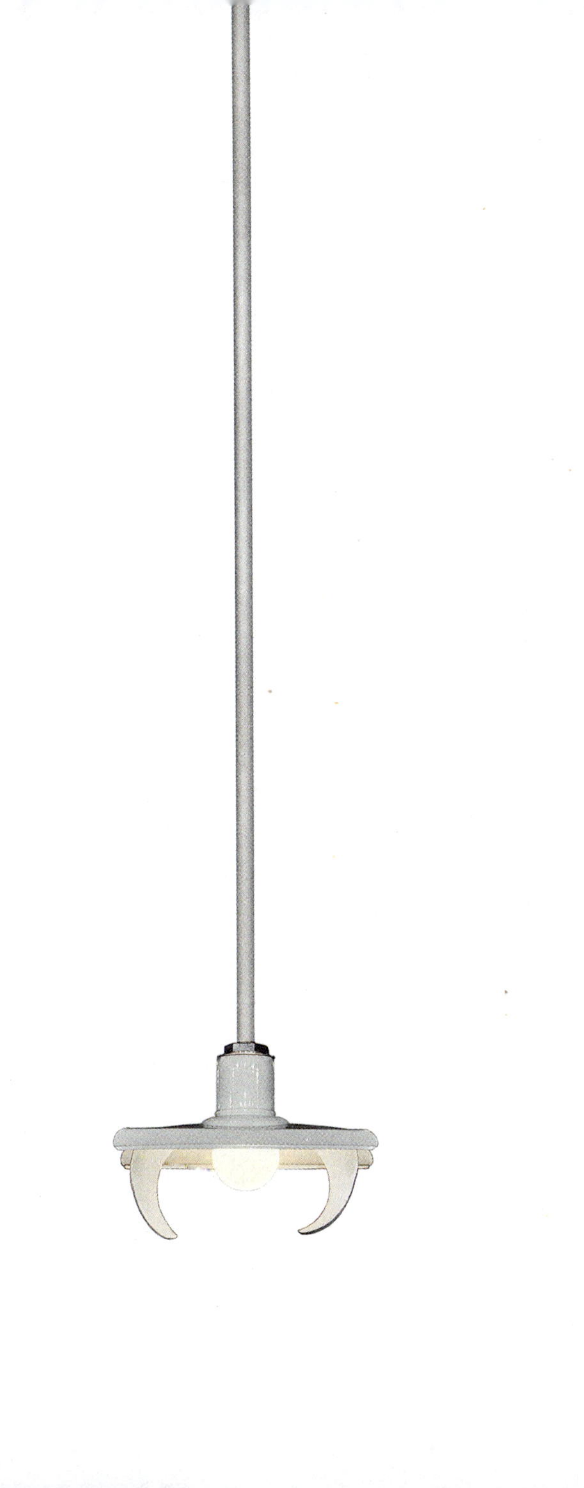

Reflective Comedy, standing shoulder wall, 2023

Spark steel or flint, oil, glass, delay, 2017–22

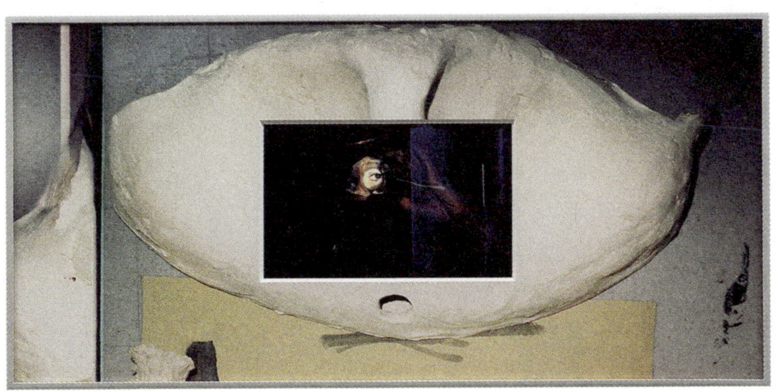

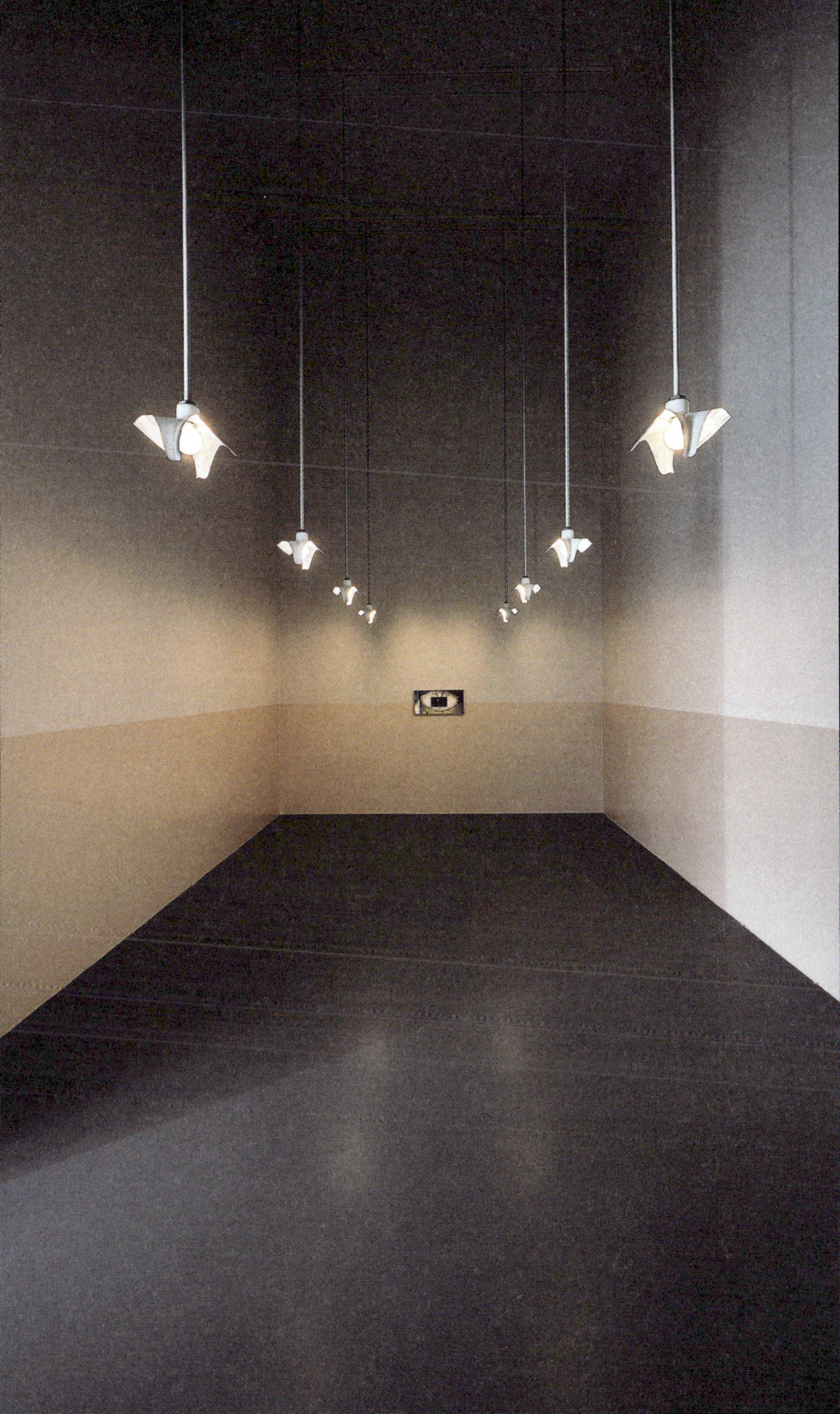

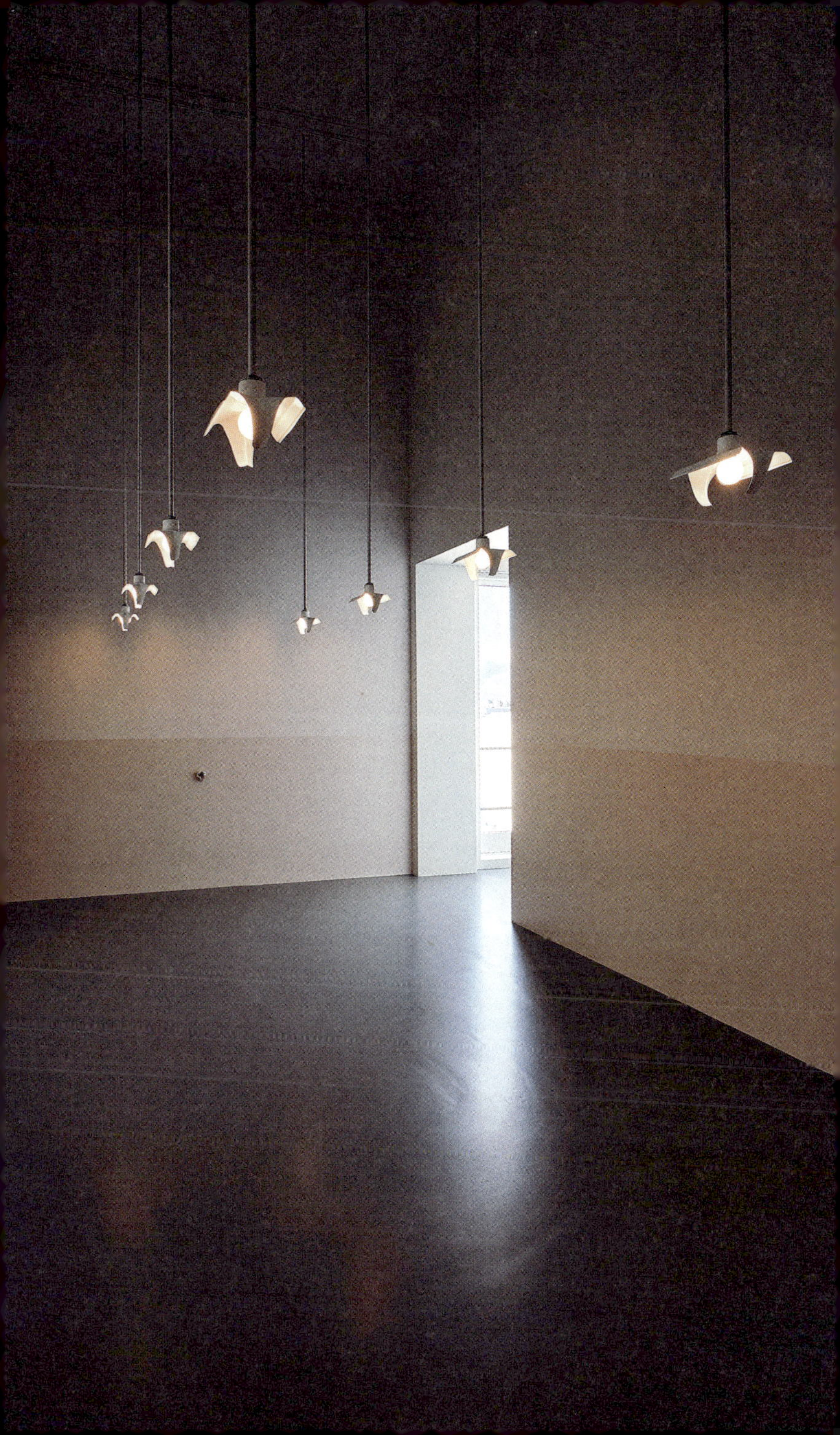

Architect's Mouth, 2022

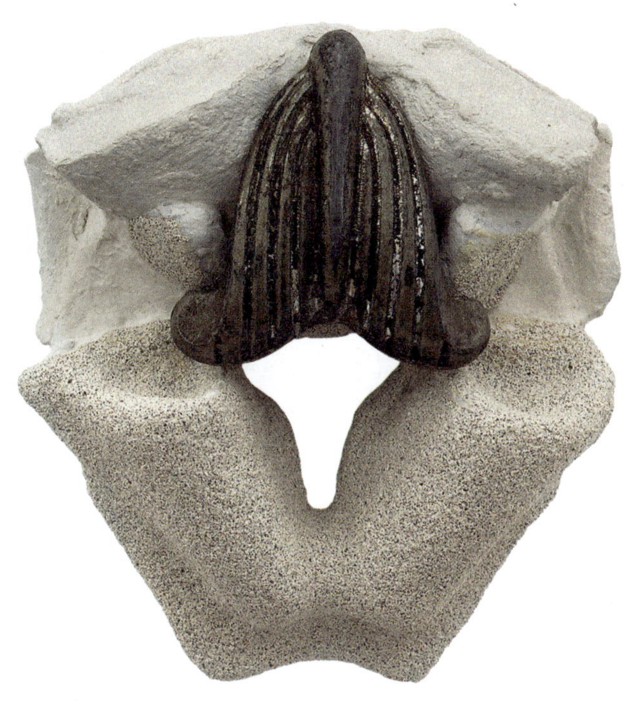

THINKING OF A TABLE WHEN I AM NOT THERE

Kate Nesin

January 20–February 20

The table is all legs, initially. Or seems so: I'm looking at a photograph, taken perhaps from a leggy angle. Eight vertical struts of square tubing with round foot pads. Three horizontal crossbars near the floor, which lead me to extrapolate another four at tabletop height, though there could be more. This framework of uniformly black metal upholds five tabletop pieces stacked like flatpack components fresh from their box—each a rectangle of thick, raw-edged particle board sandwiched between sleek scrims of black laminate. The effect is that of an abundance of legs and an abundance of tabletops, enough to make multiple tables. The particle board elements are orderly, compressed; also, technically, loose, unsecured.

This curious table structure of 2023 has a title, *Total Work (Cast of Mind)*, and its label's medium line specifies, in addition to steel, particle board, melamine laminate, glue, and screws, what B. Ingrid Olson calls "impermanent inclusions"—anything she places, for a time, on the table. During the first month of exhibition in Reykjavík, the artist's phrasing accounts for three items: the scumbled porcelain sculpture *Feminine Thought, model*, 2022–23, resting on the uppermost board; a tidy pile of two paperback books on one of the two boards just below. The books are *Occasional Works and Seven Walks from the Office for Soft Architecture* by Lisa Robertson and *The Eyes of the Skin: Architecture and the Senses* by Juhani Pallasmaa, each in its own way as compact, dense with promise, and tempting to touch as the enigmatic clay sculpture nearby.

A Total Work

The table undergirds artworks by Olson and textual works by others: a base for displaying finished work, like a plinth; a repository for the ongoing work of thinking and reading, like a desktop. The phrase "impermanent inclusions" suggests only passing contact, but because this unusual table is also an artwork (not solely a plinth, not solely a desktop), I wonder whether it absorbs some aspect of that which passes across it, every impermanent inclusion growing the work's total.

The nineteenth-century German term *Gesamtkunstwerk*, "total work of art," refers to an aesthetic ideal characterized by the synthesis of forms or modes customarily separated by discipline. The sum is meant to exceed its parts, and the concept includes an aspect of total immersion, too, as in famous architectural Gesamtkunstwerks like Frank Lloyd Wright's 1910 Robie House in Chicago, for which Wright designed not only the building but also all the furniture, fixtures, and finishes, in the interest of a fully integrated experience.

There is "total" as in whole, entire, summative, complete: This is all of it, here lies all of it.

There is "total" as in encompassing, consuming, a fullness of scope, not so much a whole anything as a voracious everything: This represents all of it, all of it can lie here.

Of course, *Total Work* is only one part of the title *Total Work (Cast of Mind)*. Parentheticals usually signal an aside or digression, yet in this case also a counter. What might seem total is in fact (only but not merely) one way of thinking, indicating a tendency or propensity, more and less fixed.

February 21–March 20

The table's components remain as before, while the impermanent inclusions change. In the place of *Feminine Thought, model* now sits *Body Parsed, Three Rooms*, 2018. A second stacked pair of books joins the first, Jorge Luis Borges's *Labyrinths* atop Renee Gladman's *Plans for Sentences*. The books share a board. The sculpture occupies a single plane yet two different boards, whose visible seam of abutment slices between what I want to call, impossibly, two unequal halves.

March 6–20

The two unequal halves of *Body Parsed, Three Rooms* swap boards for most of March, still oriented toward each other in the same way, but now the pale gray fragment of face looks blankly toward the windowed wall as well as blankly toward the two pale gray fragments of, what might these be—buttocks, crotch, upper thighs, one lap doubled, or two laps stacked?

Especially given the books Olson has placed proximately, I appreciate her titular verb "to parse," which means to analyze a sentence, breaking it down into its syntactical parts. A body's interior posited as an architectural interior, but also a body's parts posited as words (and words as containers, sometimes capacious, sometimes simply hollow).

Put another way: Here, as before, this sculpture and these books appear to offer themselves to each other as interpretive tools.

Orienteering

Yesterday my younger son asked, "Where is the back of the world and where is the front?"

March 21–April 22

Feminine Thought, model returns to its original position, replacing *Body Parsed, Three Rooms.* A new book presents itself on top of the Borges and Gladman volumes: *Architectural Body* by Madeline Gins and Shusaku Arakawa.

The sentence "Feminine thought returns" entertains me for a moment, and I wonder whether I can tell the difference between the knowing humor (conspiring, inviting) active in much of Olson's work and the eccentricity I introduce by trying to narrate through all my not-knowing. Even just by trying to narrate comprehensively (totally) certain adjustments to which I was never privy in person.

Between Two and Three Dimensions

Over the years, I've spent a fair deal of time contemplating the flattest kind of sculpture, or how flat a sculpture can be without disqualifying itself as such. This is a question that elides the in-the-round of sculptural convention with the in-between of relief, the latter typically conceived as a dimensional state that is more than two, less than three. I would argue that relief itself is a site of elision—or rather, a physical substantiation of the capacity to be two different things, to confuse two different things, to desire two different things, as well as the capacity to maintain crucial, excruciating ambivalence about the merging and annulling that nestles at the etymological heart of *elision.*[1]

Like any three-dimensional table, *Total Work (Cast of Mind)* functions in the round. Yet I think of the stacked boards of its tabletop as composing a sculptural relief in its own right as much as it participates in the composition of a larger sculpture. Typical flatpack furniture portends a future three-dimensional state, identical or near-identical pieces signifying an eventually differentiated top, bottom, sides, tiers. Olson's stack just as readily portends some future two-dimensional state, the eventual assumption of a single unrelieved plane.

Might it be possible to read all of Olson's work in relation to relief? For starters, she disclaims conventional categories, making sculptural photographs and photographic sculptures. More broadly, though, Olson's works tend to materialize precisely what is irreconcilable about two and three dimensions—the biases, errors, and lacunae that emerge in attempting to translate between them. A body imaged on paper, a floor plan imaging a room. A three-dimensional room, too, formed by the placement of two-dimensional walls. To provide a literal example that slides quickly into the imaginary: Olson prints her matting materials photographically as well as the paper they frame, so that her photographic surface—taken as a whole—includes the shallow relief of an almost paper-thin depression or impression. Paper-thin, but variously tunnel-like and deflective, so that I sometimes feel viscerally disoriented, falling into or falling away from the work.

So yes, it seems possible to read all of Olson's work as relief.[2] But the premise of this text is slightly different, if adjacent: It seems possible for a tabletop to stand in, synecdochically, for an entire exhibition. Such is my impulse, at any rate. To make *Total Work (Cast of Mind)* about all of it, and vice versa.

April 27–June 20

The invocations of readiness and futurity above were either foreshadowing or spoiler: Olson's stacking of books no longer echoes the stacking of boards, both because the books are gone and because the five laminated boards are now contiguous, arrayed to follow the table's unique framework, now more *like* a table. On account of their varying dimensions, the boards as arranged form an uninterrupted edge on one long side while making two small bays on the other, too narrow for a visitor to move into, yet inviting nevertheless. A pair of halfway invitations, well-intentioned and stymied.

The books are not gone, actually. They are stacked on a shallow preexisting shelf that runs along one wall above the radiators. By moving to the margins of this room, and to another horizontal surface (they still lie flat, have not been "shelved"), these books manage to extend the tabletop of *Total Work (Cast of Mind)* or to demonstrate its supplementation. They have increased it or distributed it, either way adding, again, to its total.

The table looks fairly full. Where the stacked books had been, *Artists Book*, 2010–23, a medium-gray picture frame encircling two rectangles of greige matboard, each of which grounds a pile of loose sheets—sketches, collages, oddments of paper—laid side by side like an open portfolio. Meanwhile, the sculpture *Liar's Envelope*, 2020–23, perplexes its own seeming openness, indeed the very idea of openness: It is about the size of a book left open to a particular page, though its pages are thick, creamy cotton overlain crosswise with curls of porcelain. Not quite blank, but wordless. Even so, this sculpture helps me think about words. About when *fold* is a verb and when it is a noun. When *open* is a verb and when it is an adjective. When *close* designates closing off and when, with a softer sibilance, it designates intimacy, being or holding near.

Beside *Liar's Envelope* lies *Clock / Painting*, 2023, a narrow papery strip—perhaps two fingers wide, one finger long—spattered and smudged with painterly residue. It is a surface that blinks with studio energy, or with studio memory, a remnant from making something else as well as, technically, itself. In hope of securing the ephemeral, a brown-headed pushpin affixes *Clock / Painting* to the table. The thought of anything piercing that smooth black tabletop shocks me, and this tiny work suddenly looms large.

The fourth impermanent inclusion, *Subject Position*, 2022–23, looks to me like a light fixture awaiting installation, resting casually yet elegantly on a sort of cupped hand of plywood and a folded square of rosy velvet. A globe light oddly attenuated, rendered more glob-like. The white fiberglass, materially, seems to contain rather than emanate light, and is also light of weight; the elongated globe shape is also a little like an elongated skull shape—a casing, evidently sutured—and I am compelled by the strangeness of an abstracted cranium aglow with subjectivity. Pulling outward, I hold onto my association of this sculpture with light because of a new work, *A small bore of light, but did it see her*, 2023, for which Olson cut a circular hole through a false wall that concealed a gallery window, revealing a flat circle of sky and initiating a volumetric shaft of light and air.[3]

Portal, Part One

In her studio, Olson keeps a table similar to that of *Total Work (Cast of Mind)*. This private working table has been preparatory, a stage for dress rehearsals as well as, presumably, a site for testing iterations that audiences will never see. As another total work it represents more work and a bigger total; which is to say, the studio table has changed more, and more often, I imagine. To be sure, it has seized my imagination. In my mind's eye, I see the table's top from above, Olson's head bowed over it. In my mind's eye, I see objects shifting noiselessly from point to point, briefly pausing to hold taut the interstices between them, before moving on again. In my mind's eye, I see these objects then vanishing, as if dropped through a trapdoor, the table's laminated expanse really a portal—direct from location of making to location of display.

A portal can mean an actual doorway or a more virtual point of entry, a website, a landing page: a means of crossing into some other realm. Olson's clearly tactile concerns belie virtuality, when virtuality is tactility's opposite. But *Total Work (Cast of Mind)* grants a sort of permission to revalue the differential intimacies of the being-in-person-with versus the being-in-mind-of.[4] Perhaps more simply, to consider the tabletop a projection of mind, representing the inputs, the transit of ideas, the habits of thought, specific in form to this artist but available structurally to others as well.[5]

May 30–June 12

Olson turns the page of *Artists Book*, so to speak, lifting the drawing from a sheaf of paper at the right and placing it face down on top of a sheaf of paper to the left. The back thus reveals a new face, which is also a solid black form that—like other works on this table—could almost be the shape of an open book, like a riddle gently proffered.

June 13–20

Olson turns the page of *Artists Book*. The left-hand page is now blank, in the sense that there is no drawing on it, only the ghostly contour of the inked figures that had appeared during the previous week as the right-hand page. Not long after, I learn that *verso*, which I have known to name, more generally, the back of a two-dimensional artwork, was first coined to name the left-hand page of an open book.

June 21–July 17

Olson turns the page of *Artists Book*. The sheet newly visible on the right looks to be the last page, or a last page, blocking whatever might lie beneath it.

July 18–31

Olson turns the page of *Artists Book*, revealing the sheaf of paper that remains. Both of the drawings that are now visible thematize doubling or mirroring, overlapping or converging—at left, two full-length back-facing figures press their sides together, standing on a single, shared leg like a stem; at right, two seemingly identical faces meet at the lips, while their noses and brows penetrate each other's profiles, imbricated. The latter imbrication is also a bleeding-through, red ink reddest where it has seeped from front to back, and this back of the drawing tendered first. (Riddling again: drawing's verso delivered as page's recto.)

August 1–28

Olson turns the page of *Artists Book*, and the doubled profile drawing now shows its front at left. As well, the luminous, bulbous *Subject Position* rotates by ninety degrees, its longer dimension now parallel with the window. *Clock / Painting* swings around the fulcrum of its round-head pin, arrowing now toward that same window.

Clock / Painting

In a 1958 statement for a journal titled *It Is*, Philip Guston writes, "Painting is a clock that sees each end of the street as the edge of the world."[6] I love this sentence, which I can parse but which I can never grasp.

Paintings are timekeepers. Certainly they are records of specific marks made by specific hands at specific times in the past, and also certainly they keep working—or can keep working—well after technical completion, aging materially, received repeatedly and distinctly over time, sometimes continuously, sometimes discontinuously. (Guston's clocks, which from ten years after this quotation onward he painted often, were mostly without numbers, hands, or both.)

If each end of the street is the edge of the world, does this make the street smaller or bigger? Is the street (painting's street) its own world, apart from the world—liminal or penumbral to it—or barreling forward to meet it? I assume Guston meant on some level to unite the first and last words of his sentence, to speak to the world that each painting constitutes. Increasingly, too, I read Guston's line as referring to a kind of scalar disorientation and the effort to resolve (intellectually, emotionally) divergent timescales. For instance, the extent to which studio time—the time of making a painting—confutes clock time; the extent to which viewing time—the time of looking at a painting—confutes clock time; the extent to which so many kinds (all kinds) of lived, experiential time confute numerical clock time.

August 15–28

Olson turns the page of *Artists Book.* The right-hand sheet is opaque, beige, and printed in large black digits with the date "1986," which happens to be the year before the artist's birth.

August 29–September 20

Olson turns the page of *Artists Book.* Around it, the table is emptier. *Liar's Envelope* occupies a more central spot, supplanting *Subject Position. Clock / Painting* persists, pinned at its initial locus.

After passing through the room in which *Total Work (Cast of Mind)* has iterated for seven months, now a visitor proceeds toward a new, related table sculpture—though one without legs, solely tabletop. *Total Work (Rest)*, 2023, consists of five rectangles of black-laminated particle board, neatly stacked like the identical boards in earlier versions of *Total Work (Cast of Mind)*. Paradoxically, Olson's choice of parenthetical term highlights the effort sometimes left latent in "work" by claiming instead a kind of resting state, as if the table's legs had folded invisibly under it, letting the floor bear the weight of its full horizontal expanse. This initial version of *Total Work (Rest)* includes as well what its boards in turn bear: *Subject Position*, maybe also resting, at a visitor's feet.

Portal, Part Two, or Beyond Three Dimensions

The contour of the assembled tabletop in *Total Work (Cast of Mind)* approximates the footprint of a particular wall with two doorways cut into it. The two recesses, or setbacks, where the table's top narrows do not replicate but palpably recollect for Olson the two thresholds that remained in regular use during the visible lifespan of her work *White Wall, painted for Gray*. That intervention, at the Carpenter Center for the Visual Arts in Cambridge, Massachusetts, transformed one of Le Corbusier's red interior walls for several months in 2022. I say "visible lifespan" because Olson's white wall persists now invisibly, beneath a fresh coat of the architect's red—not scraped or stripped away but subsumed.[7]

Once *Total Work (Rest)* had been on view in stacked form for three weeks, Olson distributed its five laminated boards to look like the continuous tabletop in *Total Work (Cast of Mind)*, though still flat on the floor: not a replica either, more like a reverberation. At a certain point, *Subject Position* was joined on this low-slung platform by its prior companions *Liar's Envelope* and *Clock / Painting*.[8] But this second iteration of *Total Work (Rest)* can be glimpsed only partially, for Olson has cleaved the room into halves, building a four-and-a-half-foot-high wall that separates the work from its viewers. A vertical window, its interior frame lined with steel, bisects this wall, the two together—aperture and barrier—comprising *Sluice (A weird rewriting of negative capability?)*, 2023. This structure asserts itself as both an inhibiting and a mediating device within the gallery. Despite its physical, regulatory presence, the wall does not foreclose the possibility of a pouring-forth, in fact pronouncing the likelihood of something intangible passing through it from artwork to viewer and, conversely, viewer to artwork. Thus *Sluice (A weird rewriting of negative capability?)* redounds to *Total Work (Rest)*, because it predicates the very surplus, or overflow, that Olson's tabletop seems built to soak up, spongelike, into its definition of totality.

Surplus and expansion feature in another way. While I forge my closing lines, I keep thinking about Olson's *Total Work* works as, ultimately, four-dimensional sculptures. By which I mean—with time assumed the fourth coordinate—to indicate change-over-time as core to their operativeness. I also mean to underscore a fundamentally human failure to experience them fully (totally): I cannot always know quite what time it is, whether for myself or for them. So much of the total remains unaccounted for. I am also saying that there is no total. Cumulativeness feels important to these works, energetically speaking, but if cumulativeness intimates remembering, surely these tabletops can forget, too. Consider as well how their relationship to dimensionality has ramified for me here, in both cases exceeding or confounding conventional bounds, from 2.5D to 4D. At heart—or, just as critically, at their limits—Olson's *Total Work* works are all potential, guarantors of more (and more and more: accrual, removal, loss, return) to come.

NOTES

A note on the title:

> *"Oh, but," said Lily, "think of his work!"*
>
> *Whenever she "thought of his work" she always saw clearly before her a large kitchen table. It was Andrew's doing. She asked him what his father's books were about. "Subject and object and the nature of reality," Andrew had said. And when she said Heavens, she had no notion what that meant. "Think of a kitchen table then," he told her, "when you're not there."*
>
> *So now she always saw, when she thought of Mr. Ramsay's work, a scrubbed kitchen table. It lodged now in the fork of a pear tree, for they had reached the orchard. And with a painful effort of concentration, she focused her mind, not upon the silver-bossed bark of the tree, or upon its fish-shaped leaves, but upon a phantom kitchen table, one of those scrubbed board tables, grained and knotted, whose virtue seems to have been laid bare by years of muscular integrity, which stuck there, its four legs in air.*

Virginia Woolf, *To the Lighthouse* (1927; New York: Harcourt Brace & Company, 1981), 23.

A note on timing:

While this text began as a calendrical log of sorts, it was not written across 2023 but rather during a few compressed autumnal weeks. A diary on delay, sequence pushed toward simultaneity—and then necessarily falling behind, too, as I only wrote according to the installation photographs available to me through September. I see now that the ways in which comprehensiveness can tip into unreadability was part of my subject matter from the start.

Notes on the text:

1. See Th. Killian Roach's thoughts on elision in Olson's work in the current volume, pages 112–17.

2. On Olson's relief works, see *B. Ingrid Olson: History Mother, Little Sister*, ed. Dan Byers and B. Ingrid Olson (Cambridge, MA: Carpenter Center for the Visual Arts, 2022), esp. Dan Byers, "Touring the Exhibitions," 10–11, and Leah Pires, "As Structure Is to Body, Body Is to Form," 66–69.

3. Notably, Olson has made multiple installations from actual found and altered light fixtures (though none so far globular), including the work in this exhibition *What I would be if I wasn't what I am, I, I*, n.d. During the weeks of *Subject Position*'s initial appearance in the adjoining gallery, *What I would be if I wasn't what I am, I, I* depended from the ceiling

next door, lighting its long, dim room with the minor but vivid aid of another hole in the wall—a second instance of *A small bore of light, but did it see her* simultaneous with the first.

4. Dan Byers has written aptly of the "Cartesian joke" at work: "The mind, especially as it sees, is perhaps the most bodily part of Olson's practice." Byers, "Touring the Exhibitions," 11.

5. An otherwise curious historical reference becomes an irresistible one, given these terms of projection, passage, and portal: The notion of tables that behave surprisingly, tables that mediate, can be found in the mid-nineteenth century in spiritist practices variously known as table turning, table tapping, table tipping, or table tilting, described for instance in a contemporaneous book by Justinus Kerner called *The Somnambulent Tables* (Stuttgart: Ebner and Seubert, 1853). More than a decade later, Karl Marx evoked such eerie behaviors with a difference, reinforcing the "metaphysical subtleties" of the commodity by providing the image of a table turned "on its head [to] evolve out of its wooden brain grotesque ideas, far more wonderful than if it were to begin dancing of its own free will." Karl Marx, *Capital*, vol. 1, *A Critique of Political Economy*, trans. Ben Fowkes (New York: Penguin, 1976), 163–64.

6. This line concludes a short statement reprinted in *Philip Guston: Collected Writings, Lectures, and Conversations*, ed. Clark Coolidge (Berkeley: University of California Press, 2011), 19.

7. Thanks to the artist for sharing the formal connection between her painted wall intervention and her subsequent table works. B. Ingrid Olson, email to the author, October 10, 2023.

8. Other changes introduced by the end of October were a new *Subject Position* as well as a new *Clock / Painting*, the latter strip still slight but almost twice as long as Olson's first—its papery yellow ground more visible, above and below prominent smudges of silver gouache. The pin at one end is tiny, with a flat head, a metal stickpin. Two subject positions in one exhibition might automatically indicate differentiation. Two clocks, likewise?

Iteration II

February 21–March 20, 2023

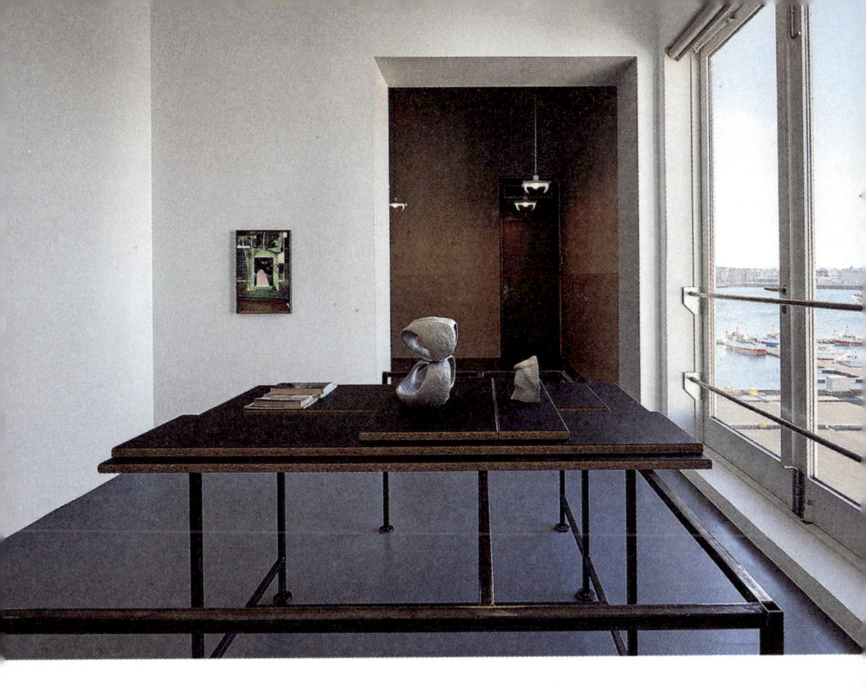

Rifted Grid, per fluid, 2021–22

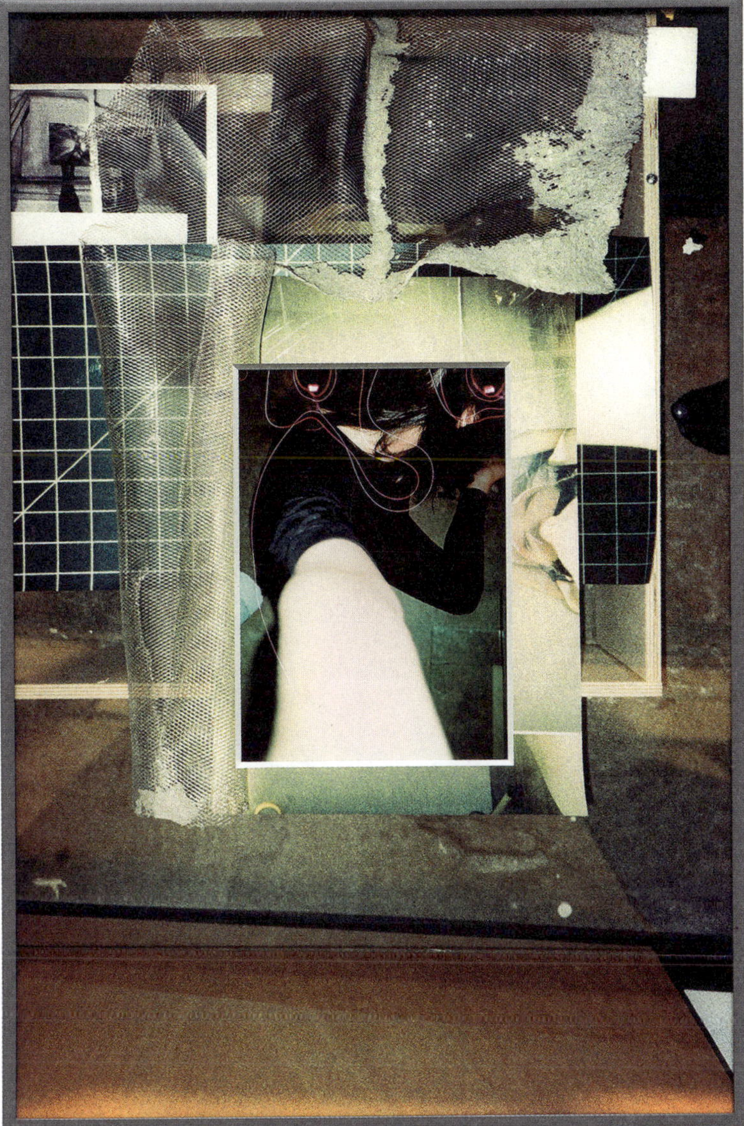

Body Parsed, Three Rooms, 2018

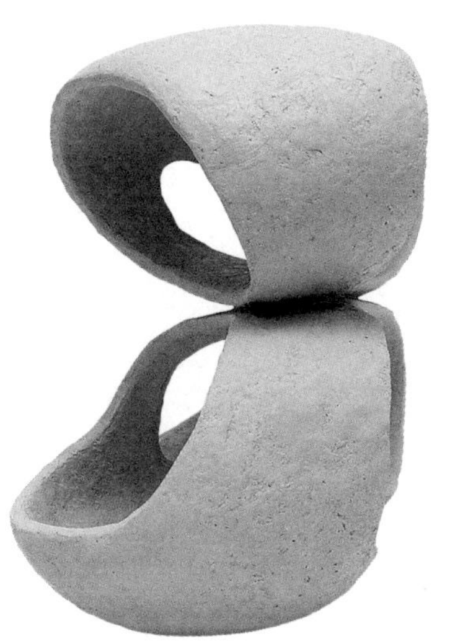

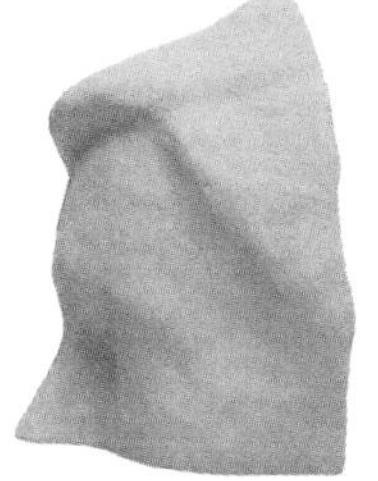

Introductions by Kate Zambreno (replica), 2018/2023

FOREHEAD AND BRAIN

I realized I was extremely miserable when I wrote the previous introduction. Now I am extremely happy. Or perhaps I was happy the entire time. I read a paragraph and then have to rest. I lie down on the sofa. I lay the book down. I lay myself down because I am now the book. I write a sentence and then have to check my email. After I write I am hollowed out. Do I even have a brain. I put the book up to my forehead and lay it on my brain. I put the book on my crotch and take a photograph. I wonder whether the book is a container, and what it is a container for. Perhaps it is a container for thoughts. Perhaps it is a container for language. Perhaps it is a container for memory. It is something like a brain. Is the mind a room. I spend time looking at images of the illustrations of the brain from Vesalius's The Fabric of the Human Body. I want to write about the Dark Room of this Book, furnished with a stretched cloth. A frame with cloth stretched over it is a painting. A frame with cloth stretched over it is a body. A frame with a cloth stretched over it is a window or a table. The body is a house. Vesalius was one of the first to dissect human beings in a surgical theater, not just animals as before, because of religion. He dissected the brains of convicts, most likely. He thought there was just fluid in the ventricles, not the soul like everyone else. Medical illustrations want to make the body an open window, so we can see the structures within. What is a skull but a vitrine for the brain. What occupies the theater of the forehead is the front matter, the dura, the folds. Now we know something of what the cerebral cortex stores, in future mappings of the frontal lobes: movement, speech, memory, intelligence. I look at an illustration of his horizontal dissection of the brain. The strange illustration of the man with the beard and nose, his head hollowed, like he is awake or surprised.

FOREHEAD AND BRAIN

I realized I was extremely miserable when I wrote the previous introduction. Now I am extremely happy. Or perhaps I was happy the entire time. I read a paragraph and then have to rest. I lie down on the sofa. I lay the book down. I lay myself down because I am now the book. I write a sentence and then have to check my email. After I write I am hollowed out. Do I even have a brain. I put the book up to my forehead and lay it on my brain. I put the book on my crotch and take a photograph. I wonder whether the book is a container, and what it is a container for. Perhaps it is a container for thoughts. Perhaps it is a container for language. Perhaps it is a container for memory. It is something like a brain. Is the mind a room. I spend time looking at images of the illustrations of the brain from Vesalius's The Fabric of the Human Body. I want to write about the Dark Room of this Book, furnished with a stretched cloth. A frame with cloth stretched over it is a painting. A frame with cloth stretched over it is a body. A frame with a cloth stretched over it is a window or a table. The body is a house. Vesalius was one of the first to dissect human beings in a surgical theater, not just animals as before, because of religion. He dissected the brains of convicts, most likely. He thought there was just fluid in the ventricles, not the soul like everyone else. Medical illustrations want to make the body an open window, so we can see the structures within. What is a skull but a vitrine for the brain. What occupies the theater of the forehead is the front matter, the dura, the folds. Now we know something of what the cerebral cortex stores, in future mappings of the frontal lobes: movement, speech, memory, intelligence. I look at an illustration of his horizontal dissection of the brain. The strange illustration of the man with the beard and nose, his head hollowed, like he is awake or surprised.

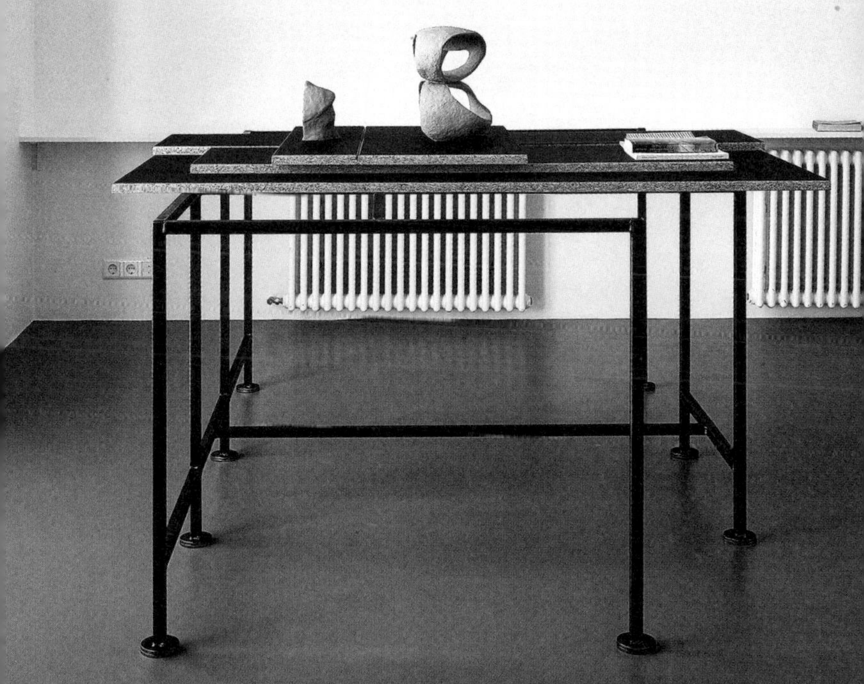

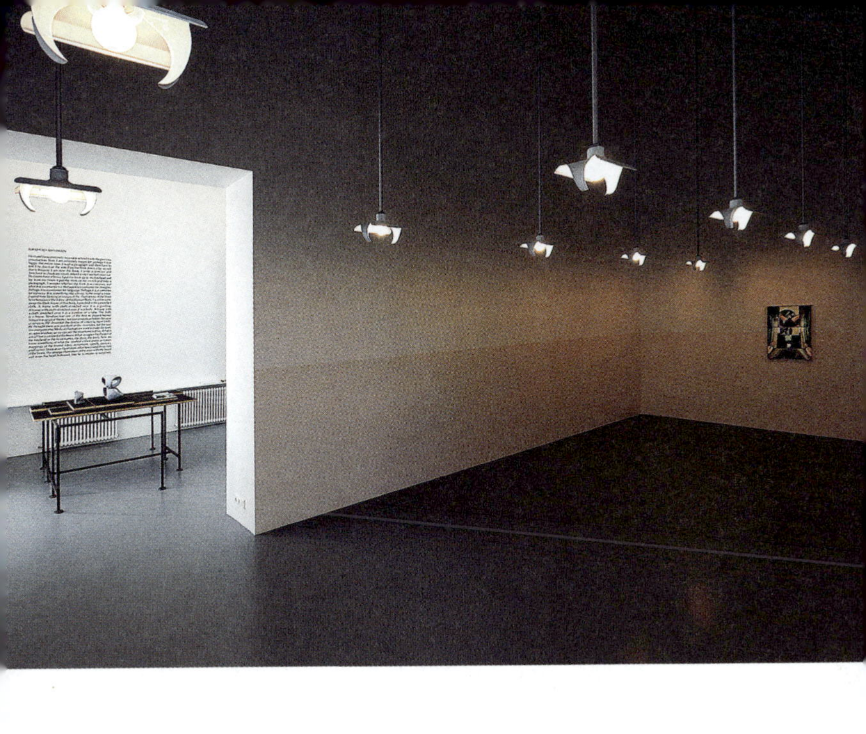

Coming in with your back turned, 2021–22

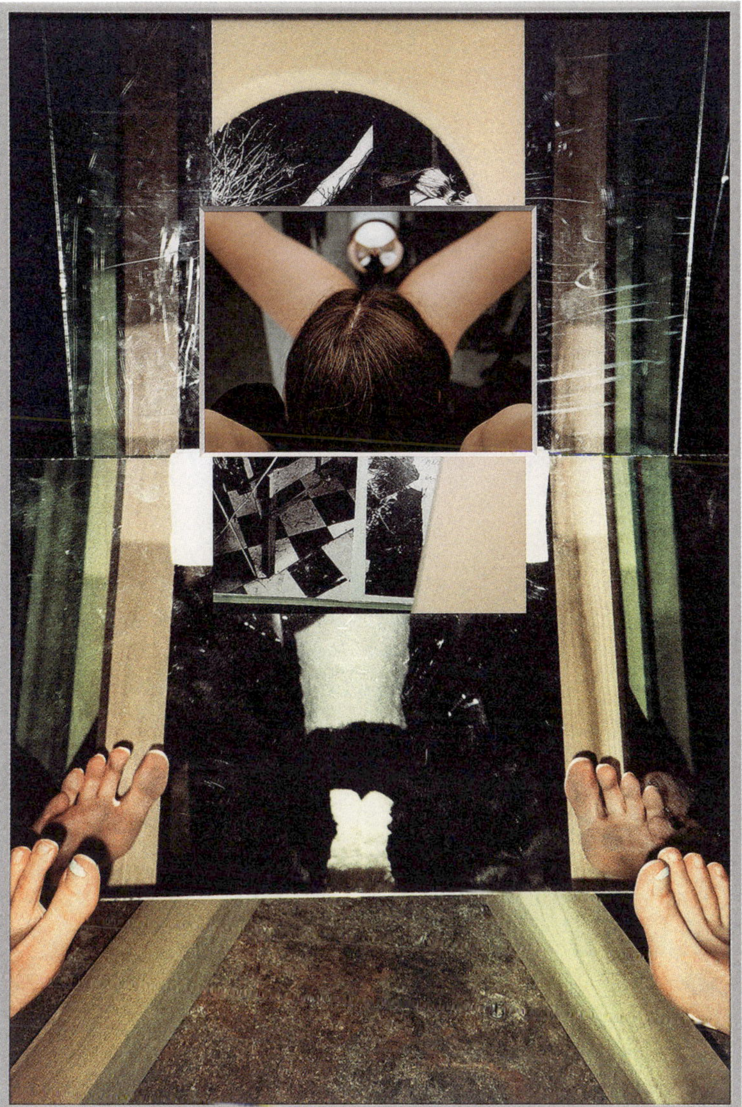

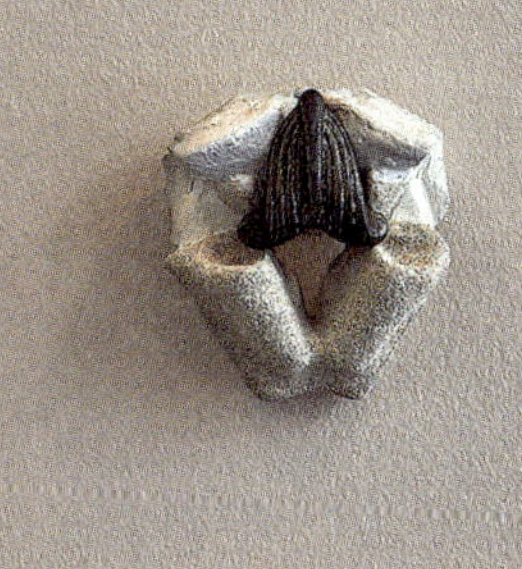

March 6–20

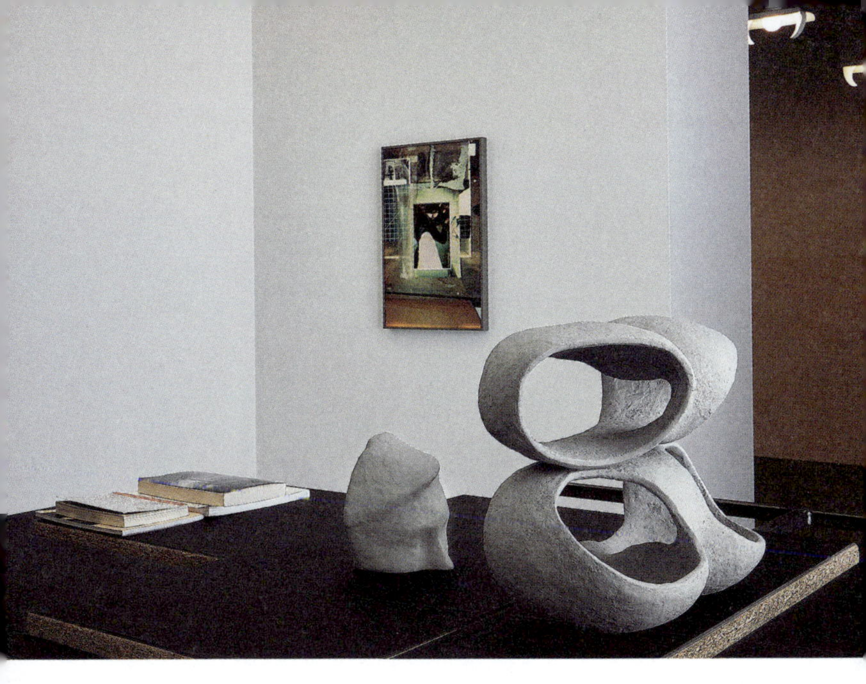

A MIRROR HELPS

Leslie Meredith Wilson

All the fixins. I want all of them.

Fixing is photography's foundation—the victory of permanence . . . sort of.[1] After so many devices had brought us close—we might pluck *handmaidens*[2] from the cornucopia of troublesome metaphors used for the helpers toward image perfection, endurance, and stability with glass, holes, dark rooms, surfaces convex and concave, mirrors, baths, patience—photography delivered something all at once lasting and fragile, less fully present, and more of a painfully slow exit.[3]

Photography is awkward.

But we can help it—bless its heart. We can dress it up just so. Conserve it. Fix the fixing.

We can mend and correct and keep dead things dead again.

We do it to cats and dogs. Fix them. Stop their reproduction.

We stop.

In parts of the American South, fixing—in all of its delicious variations in form, from fixin' to finna—means planning to do something. It's an engine revving up. It's about to go down.

Fixins are accompaniments. The good stuff that goes with the main. The strong supporting cast. Ensemble magic.

Fixings are things fastened to other things.

Fixes are cravings temporarily sated.

Rushes. Releases.

They are resolutions.

They don't last.

Attention—fix it—by turning to look and think like you really mean it.

Still yet, there is the sense of arranging, of making a way for. That can be a whole job. The Fixer—one who does the work of fixing, the occupation of a go-between.

Fixers are specialists in context. Familiar with the surroundings, they solve problems, make connections, translate, deal, cope. Some of them are managers of scandal, seeking angles, spinning on behalf of others. Some are cleanup crews for disasters, minor and major. They are in it up to their necks.

Or maybe it's not a neck but a shoulder. In Herbert Bayer's 1932 photomontage *Humanly Impossible (Self-Portrait)*, the artist/designer/architect/teacher appears to hold a prime cut of where his arm once joined his torso. Instead of bloody carnage, this cleavage has left a smooth, opaque surface that suggests that the artist might be made of stone, entirely or in part. Or maybe wood.[4] Or maybe plaster. He was, or he is, or he is becoming sculpture. This fact appears to be news to Bayer. The artist convincingly performs surprise, shock, horror, awe. Eyes wide, mouth open, Bayer is transfixed by what shouldn't be happening. A mirror helps.

But for mirrors to help, we often have to look in special, more attentive ways. We have to think carefully about what they do. If we forget about their reversals and distortions, mirrors remind us of these properties, perhaps, when we reach up to adjust a hair out of place and find ourselves thinking one way and feeling another. Maybe we have to watch our movements for a few more seconds to make our seeing and feeling align.

Although Bayer's amazed expression and newly suspended limb are central to *Humanly Impossible (Self-Portrait)*, I keep going back to the edges of the mirror, pictured at a slight tilt, slicing across the top and the right side of the image. This picture is itself made of cuts—cutting and photographing and retouching. I linger at the mirror's end, the move from reflective surface to the space of the room, the interplay of seams and seamlessness.[5]

I linger at mirrors' ends in B. Ingrid Olson's photographic work *Coming in with your back turned*, 2021–22. I study edges to try to figure out fronts and backs. At first, I think of a kaleidoscope, as if what I am seeing is a pause in shape-shifting. In reflecting light, the mirrors in this work offer up architectural details, the undersides of feet, and sculptural forms that defy easy description, but they are also smudged and scratched and marked. They return images but are also emphatically things assembled in a room somewhere.

The stacked and tilted mirrors in *Coming in with your back turned* were what got me thinking of Bayer in the first place. But it wasn't his self-portrait I was conjuring, rather the diagram he published in 1937 of an expanded field of vision in which a besuited figure looks at a series of flat planes around him simultaneously with the help of a single eye for a head. Represented as male and bourgeois, this figure stands in for an exhibition viewer—all exhibition viewers—looking at the many elements of a dynamic display all at once.[6] Bayer was deeply interested in the "we" who look at exhibitions, at architecture, at environments. Reaching for universal theories of perception, he sought to create exhibition designs that could "penetrate" spectators with lasting effect.[7] But then there was also Bayer in his self-portrait fixing himself into an impossible self through cutting and retouching and rephotographing, reveling in his own astonishment at what his particular body could become.

The title *Coming in with your back turned*—a phrase sliced by Olson from another somewhere—invites a tangent. It's a trope in many a thirty-minute sitcom or 120-minute romantic comedy for a groom to enter a room backward as the bride-to-be wears the white dress that is not supposed to be seen until the ceremony. The groom turns the wrong way round to stay on the right side of luck for both of their sakes.

Instead of a groom trying not to look at a bride, *Coming in with your back turned* appears to show—within an interior image bordered by the beveled edge of a matboard—the back of a person's head looking toward some parts of someone, or maybe even herself. Above and below this view, I spy parts of a black-and-white image from Marcel Duchamp's *Manual of Instructions for the Assembly of Étant donnés: 1º la chute d'eau, 2º le gaz d'éclairage* (1966), scenes from Duchamp's planning of his peep show tableau.[8] Above: a semicircle framing a cluster of skinny branches, a wig, and other elements of the assemblage-in-formation extending into a room. Below: a checkerboard floor and the leg of a table. Therefore, it is as if the scene framed within the matboard rested atop the absent (cut-out) table—this central image is the table. It looks like an examination room. A head appears as if it has converged with a vector of thighs, at the center of which is a small circular form emanating light. The fact that this view features the artist's head and the artist's foreshortened and compressed body parts matters insofar as it is specific. This is and isn't her. Olson has used herself to get in the way.

She fixed it.

It's better now.

Duchamp's assemblage-in-progress for *Étant donnés* was composed for eventual display on the other side of heavy doors into which two small holes were incised—just right for binocular vision. The photograph from Duchamp's studio that Olson invokes in *Coming in with your back turned* is a document of Duchamp figuring out what he wanted other people to look at while being looked at from behind. Olson has intervened in that process by simultaneous excision and insertion. Into a scene destined to be spied on, Olson places a head already looking from inside of a room. And it's a performance of looking that seems to demand bodily contortion, even discomfort, to find just this view. Looking costs.

If *Coming in with your back turned* were an ethic—beyond a title—it would suggest a way to move through the world looking the wrong way. If a fix is also a form of corruption in service of a desired outcome, a setup, a foregone conclusion, a rigging, then entering backward could be a means for announcing a new way to play a game. Enter backward to engage a more expansive framework for perception. Linger at mirror's ends. Confuse rectos and versos. Freestyle. Don't fix a thing.

NOTES

1. William Henry Fox Talbot refers to photography as "the art of fixing a shadow" in his foundational text *Some Account of the Art of Photogenic Drawing, or the Process by Which Natural Objects May Be Made to Delineate Themselves without the Aid of the Artist's Pencil* (London: R. and J. E. Taylor, 1839). He explains, "We may receive on paper the fleeting shadow, arrest it there, and in the space of a single minute fix it there so firmly as to be no more capable of change, even if thrown back into the sunbeam from which it derived its origin" (5). This phrase was key to how Talbot articulated his efforts to create permanent images by means of "a fixing process to prevent the further action of light upon sensitive paper." William Henry Fox Talbot, "A Brief Historical Sketch of the Invention of the Art," in *The Pencil of Nature* (London: Longman, Brown, Green, and Longmans, 1844–46), n.p.

2. The term *handmaiden* is used in influential nineteenth-century essays on photography, including texts by Lady Elizabeth Eastlake and Peter Henry Emerson. Charles Baudelaire deployed the word *servante* especially memorably when he lamented the encroachment of photography on the arts. As translated by Jonathan Mayne, he writes, "If photography is allowed to supplement art in some of its functions, it will soon have supplanted or corrupted it altogether, thanks to the stupidity of the multitude which is its natural ally. It is time . . . for it to return to its true duty, which is to be a servant of the sciences and arts—but the very humble servant, like printing or shorthand, which have neither created nor supplemented literature." Some translations use *handmaiden* in place of *servant*, indicating the feminine form of the word used by Baudelaire. Charles Baudelaire, "The Modern Public and Photography," in *Art in Paris 1845–1862* (London: Phaidon, 1965), 154 [first appeared in *Le Boulevard*, September 14, 1862]. For more on this term in the context of the gendering of aspects of photographic practice, see Harriet Riches, "'Picture taking and picture making': Gender Difference and the Historiography of Photography," in *Photography, History, Difference*, ed. Tanya Sheehan (Hanover, NH: Dartmouth College Press, 2015), 128–50.

3. I'm thinking especially of Kate Palmer Albers's excellent recent book *The Night Albums*, in which she reaches to some of photography's earliest and most recent practices to ask: "How might an engagement with photography shift if the activity of looking was understood as a fleeting experience, performative in nature?" Albers contends, "An assumption of flux, rather than permanence, shifts that experience, as does attention to a range of existence, from visible to invisible, or the reverse, from invisible to visible." Kate Palmer Albers, *The Night Albums: Visibility and the Ephemeral Photograph* (Berkeley: University of California Press, 2021), 10.

4. As suggested in Matthew S. Witkovsky, "Face Time," in *Object:Photo: Modern Photographs; The Thomas Walther Collection 1909–1949*, ed. Mitra Abbaspour, Lee Ann Daffner, and Maria Morris Hambourg, an online project of the Museum of Modern Art, 2014, https://www.moma.org/interactives/objectphoto/objects/83703.html#essays.

5. Lee Ann Daffner and Roxana Marcoci, "Herbert Bayer, Humanly Impossible," in *Object:Photo*, https://www.moma.org/interactives/objectphoto/objects/83703.html#recto.

6. I hadn't paid much attention to how that figure was coded as male up to now, but as I took to heart Gordon Hall's finely tuned analysis of the discourse of "the body" and Leah Pires's sensitive engagement with Hall's argument in relation to Olson's work in *B. Ingrid Olson: History Mother, Little Sister*, ed. Dan Byers and B. Ingrid Olson (Cambridge, MA: Carpenter Center for the Visual Arts, 2022), I think anew of the gendering of Bayer's spectator and his "eye." As an expression, "the eye" is yet another realm of collapse, as it implies that there is a normative way of looking, standard and predetermined. A generalization in service of assessing broad truths—important work, no doubt—"the eye" does not account for variations in access, experience, context, physicality, and a constellation of other factors that determine how different people look at the world. So here, "we," maybe, are helped by thinking of Bayer's eyes, wide open, staring in amazement at the reflection of his body doing something that it shouldn't be able to do—with the aid of photomontage. See Gordon Hall, "Why I Don't Talk about 'The Body': A Polemic," *Monday Journal* 4 (March 2020): 95–107; and Leah Pires, "As Structure Is to Body, So Body Is to Form," in Byers and Olson, *B. Ingrid Olson: History Mother, Little Sister*, 65–79.

7. Herbert Bayer, "Fundamentals of Exhibition Design," *PM* (December 1939–January 1940): 17–25, New York Public Library Digital Collections, https://digitalcollections.nypl.org/items/90F27111-9714-4fc1-e040-e00a18064ba4. For more on Bayer's diagram and his aims for exhibition design, see Fred Turner, "The Family of Man and the Politics of Attention in Cold War America," *Public Culture* 24, no. 1 (Winter 2012): 55–84; and Kristie La, "'Enlightenment, Advertising, Education, Etc.': Herbert Bayer and the Museum of Modern Art's 'Road to Victory,'" *October* 150 (Fall 2014): 63–86.

8. Many thanks to Phil Taylor and B. Ingrid Olson for helping me see this, and for generously sharing their feedback and insights along the way.

Iteration III

March 21–April 22, 2023

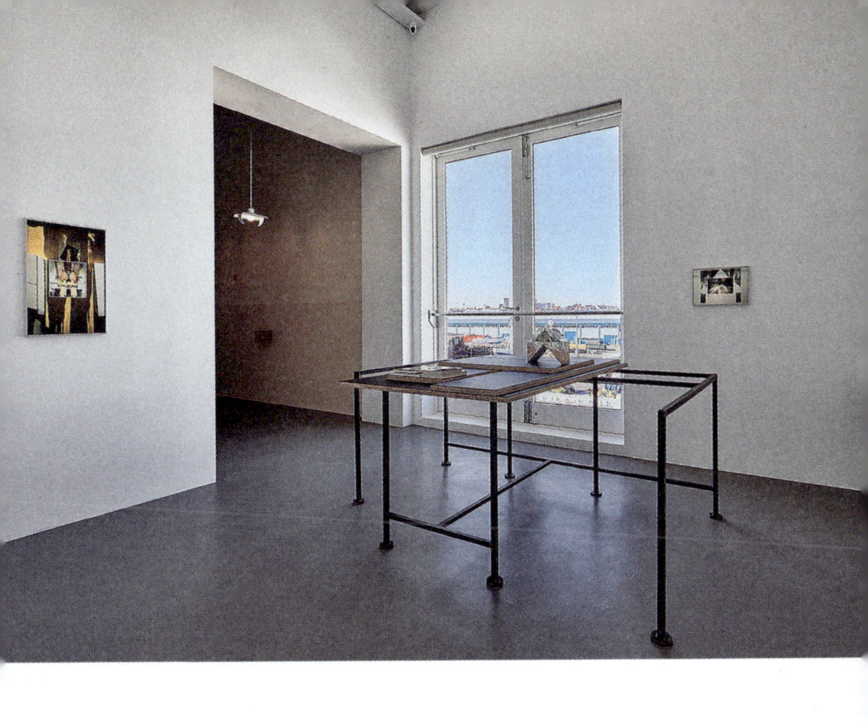

Underpinning, a twitch of glass, a pinch in the cloth, 2019–20

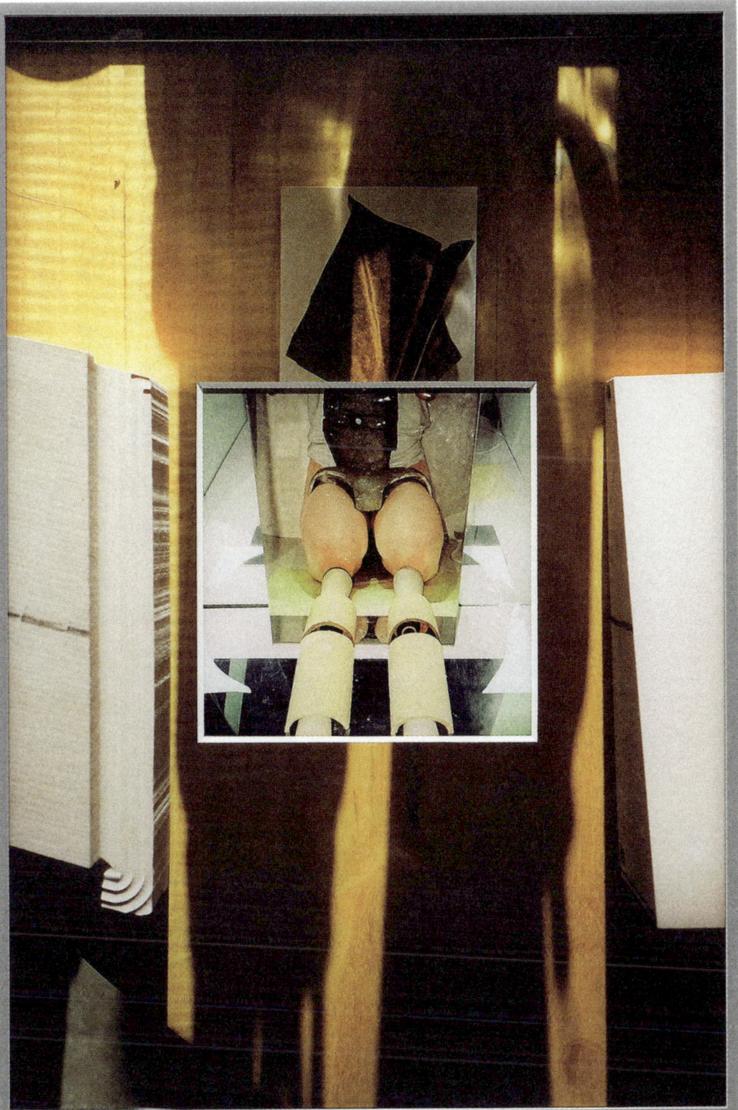

place mo
at his de

I go back
and cann
this quot
as the boo
5th floor
been dea
thought t
ones are
moved to
looking t

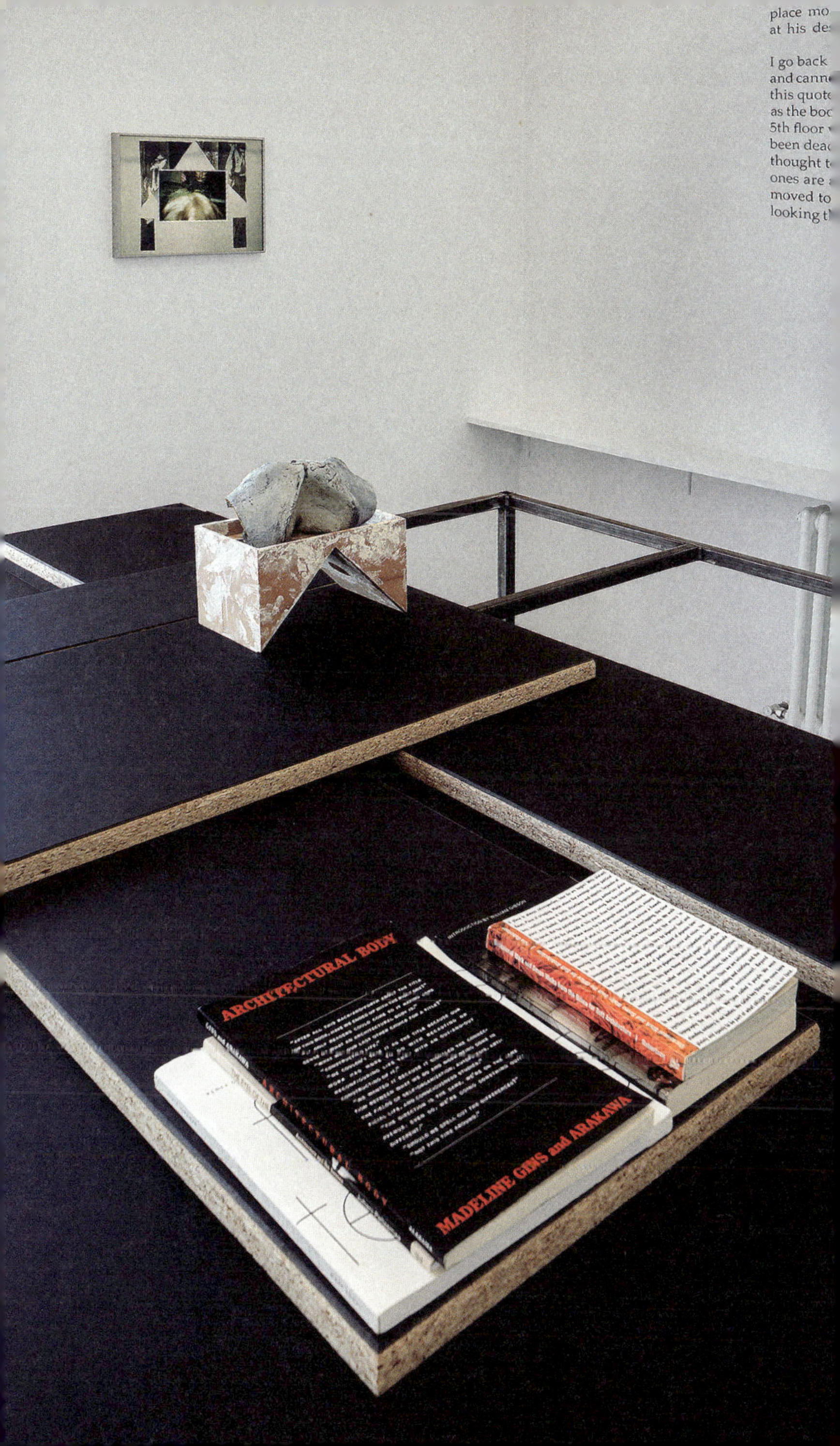

Feminine Thought, model, 2022–23

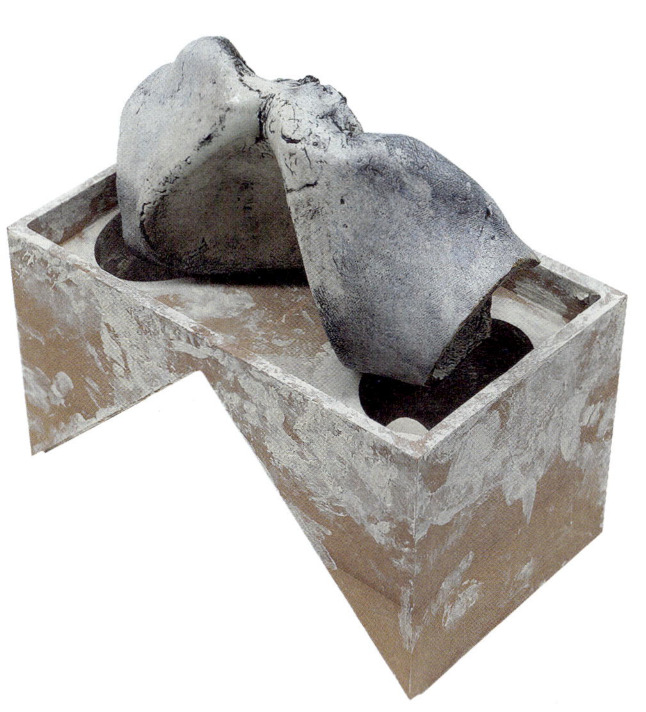

Below and Throw, 2020–21

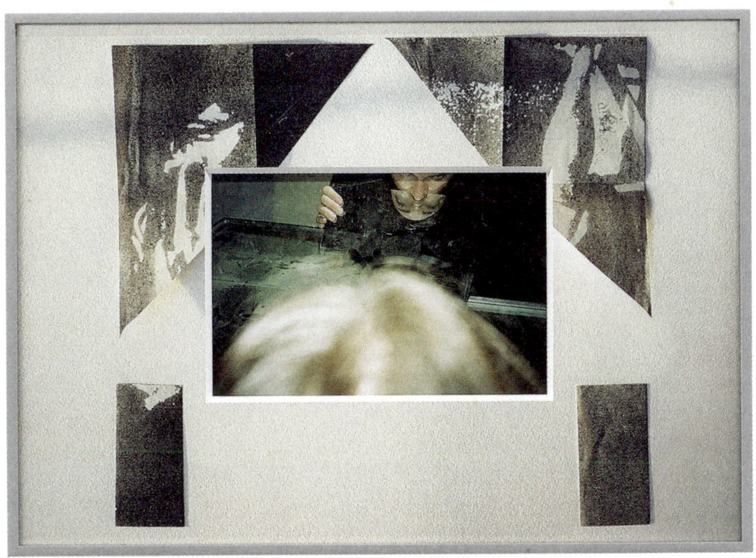

UNHINGE NAME TURNS MEMBRANE, BODY TO COME

When the question is raised of writing an introduction, one thinks that the books that need introductions are those that are opaque, and are thus impertinent to introduce. This is supposed to be an entrance or window. I wanted to have four cells on this page. Four cells would be a grid or window. The book is a dark room entitled *New Essays*. I wanted this writing to be all interior. The self must be more than what is inside and outside. What is not the self.

When writing *The Passion of GH* Clarice Lispector was going through difficulties in her family life, but the work eludes the autobiographical. It is only of a faceless woman alone in the room. She is frustrated by this "room." What can contain her. What is "narrative." What is "I." What is a "book." Who is to say. The room is unstable and becomes the narrator. "Before I entered the room, what was I?" G.H. asks. "I was what others had always seen me be, and that was the way I knew myself." When she enters her maid's room, she observes that the room was the portrait of an empty stomach. She enters into a dialogue with a cockroach which she decapitates with a door, then ultimately ingests its oozing entrails. One must ideally stand up when reading this. A text must be vertical, and should be ingested within the body.

Over the period of hours that I have written this introduction I have lost my body, my human frame. Franz Kafka wrote his story "The Judgment" in one sitting from September 22 through September 23, 1912, from 10pm to 6am. He writes in his diary that his leg grew so stiff from sitting over that 8-hour period that he had to physically pull them out from under the desk, like he had been cut in two. He felt, he wrote, such a fearful joy like the language came out of him so freely, like he was advancing over water, like he was not even a body. The story "The Judgment" takes place mostly in two separate rooms, the father is in bed, and the son is at his desk, and he goes back and forth, and they flow into each other.

I go back to my book. The psychotic person has their boundaries collapsed, and cannot distinguish between outside and inside, self and other. I have read this quoted in another introduction, because it is not likely you have read it, as the book is out of print. When Shulamith Firestone was found dead in her 5th floor walk-up in the East Village, the authorities thought she might have been dead for some time, but her family did not permit an autopsy. She was thought to have a version of Capgras Syndrome, where one fears that loved ones are actually doubles, wearing masks of the former's face. When I first moved to New York City, I would walk to her apartment and stand outside, looking through the window, and sometimes would stay there for some time.

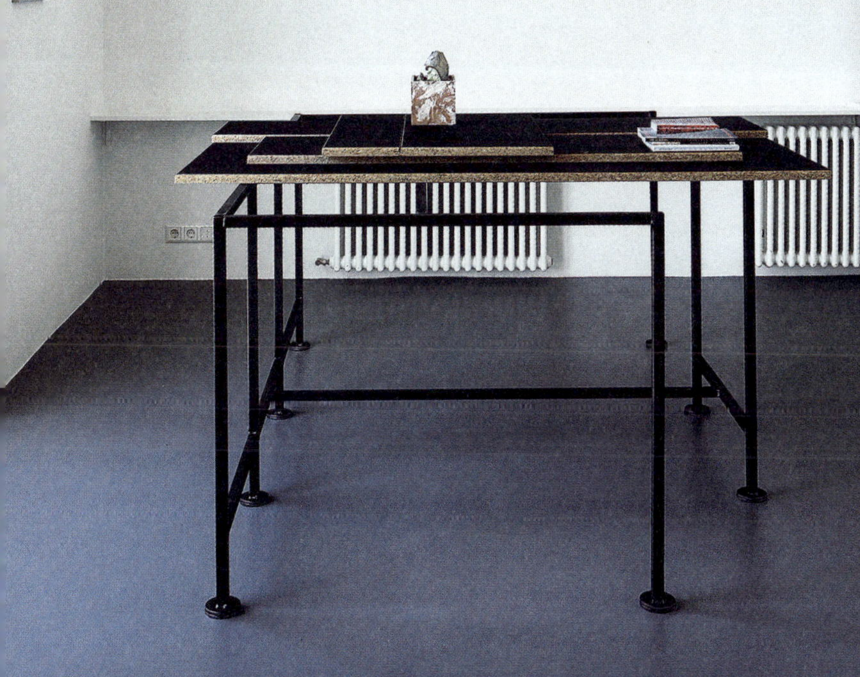

Introductions by Kate Zambreno (replica), 2018/2023

UNHINGE NAME TURNS MEMBRANE, BODY TO COME

When the question is raised of writing an introduction, one thinks that the books that need introductions are those that are opaque, and are thus impertinent to introduce. This is supposed to be an entrance or window. I wanted to have four cells on this page. Four cells would be a grid or window. The book is a dark room entitled *New Essays*. I wanted this writing to be all interior. The self must be more than what is inside and outside. What is not the self.

When writing *The Passion of GH* Clarice Lispector was going through difficulties in her family life, but the work eludes the autobiographical. It is only of a faceless woman alone in the room. She is frustrated by this "room." What can contain her. What is "narrative." What is "I." What is a "book." Who is to say. The room is unstable and becomes the narrator. "Before I entered the room, what was I?" G.H. asks. "I was what others had always seen me be, and that was the way I knew myself." When she enters her maid's room, she observes that the room was the portrait of an empty stomach. She enters into a dialogue with a cockroach which she decapitates with a door, then ultimately ingests its oozing entrails. One must ideally stand up when reading this. A text must be vertical, and should be ingested within the body.

Over the period of hours that I have written this introduction I have lost my body, my human frame. Franz Kafka wrote his story "The Judgment" in one sitting from September 22 through September 23, 1912, from 10pm to 6am. He writes in his diary that his leg grew so stiff from sitting over that 8-hour period that he had to physically pull them out from under the desk, like he had been cut in two. He felt, he wrote, such a fearful joy like the language came out of him so freely, like he was advancing over water, like he was not even a body. The story "The Judgment" takes place mostly in two separate rooms, the father is in bed, and the son is at his desk, and he goes back and forth, and they flow into each other.

I go back to my book. The psychotic person has their boundaries collapsed, and cannot distinguish between outside and inside, self and other. I have read this quoted in another introduction, because it is not likely you have read it, as the book is out of print. When Shulamith Firestone was found dead in her 5th floor walk-up in the East Village, the authorities thought she might have been dead for some time, but her family did not permit an autopsy. She was thought to have a version of Capgras Syndrome, where one fears that loved ones are actually doubles, wearing masks of the former's face. When I first moved to New York City, I would walk to her apartment and stand outside, looking through the window, and sometimes would stay there for some time.

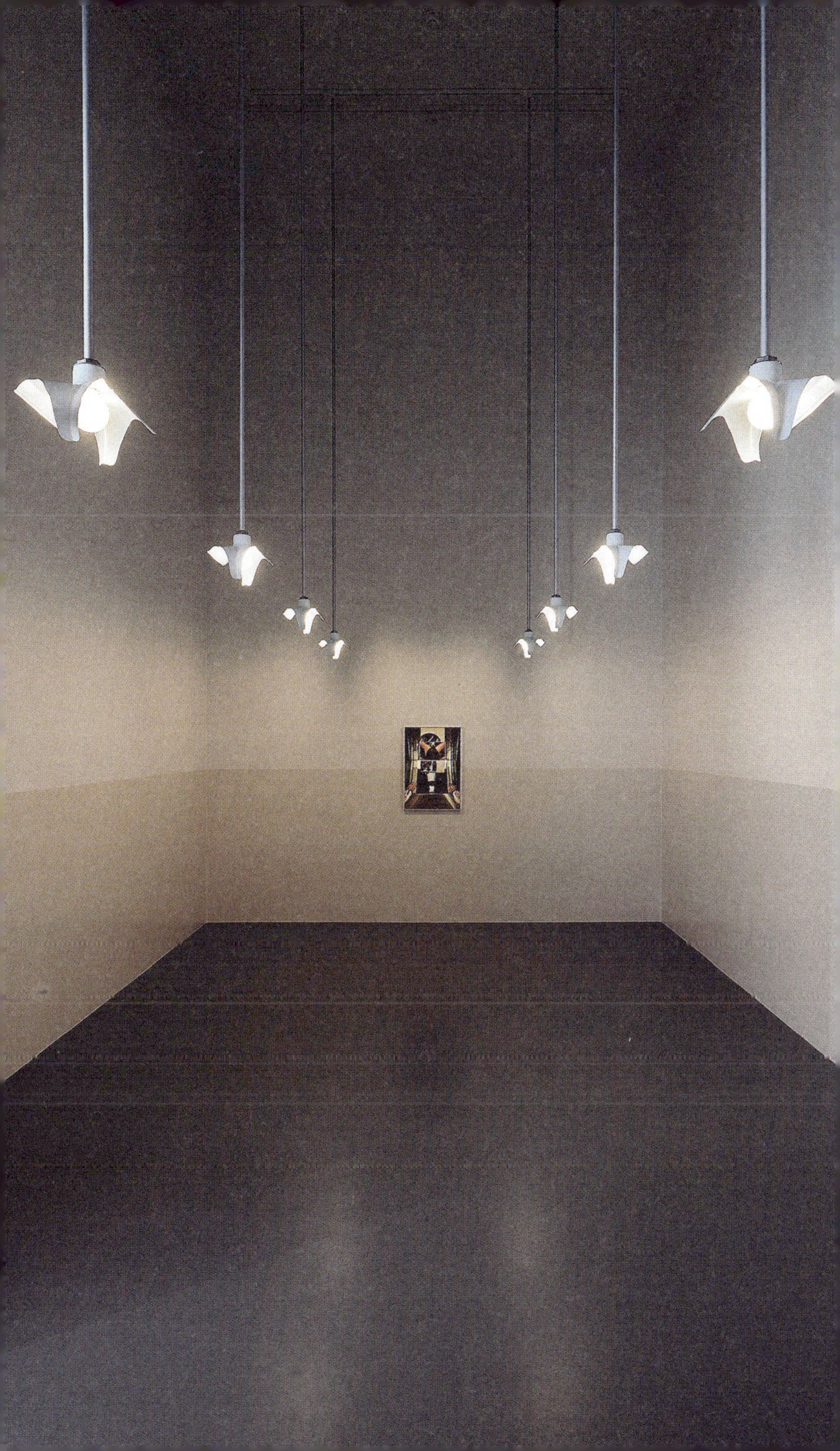

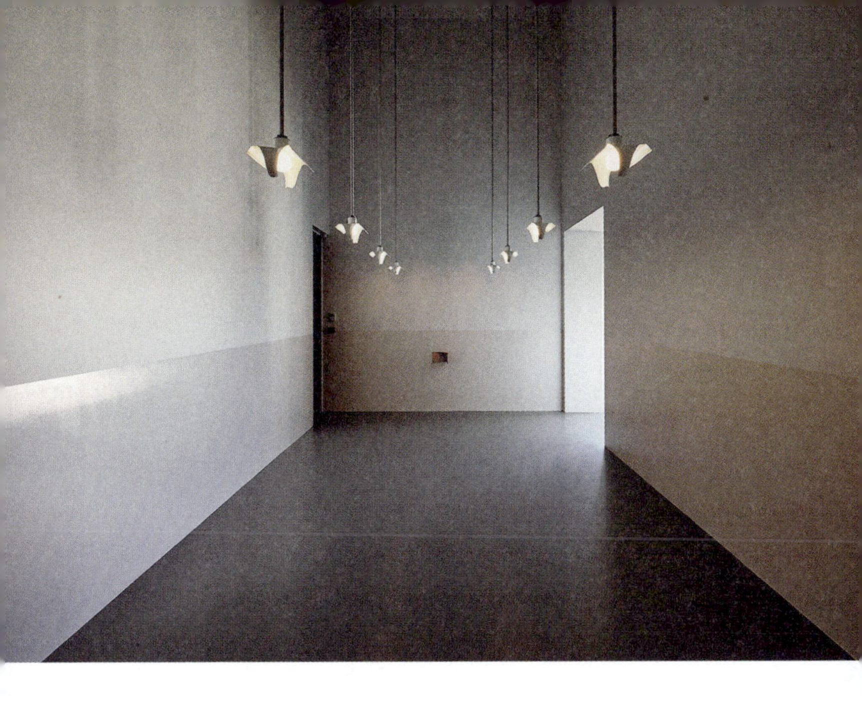

Endless House, plastic drawing, 2017

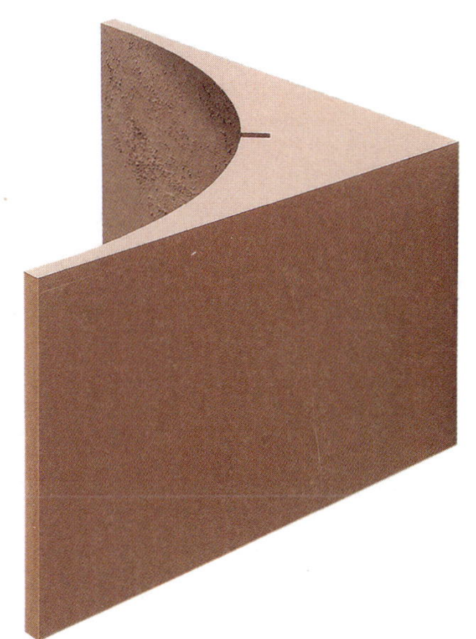

ELISIONS

Th. Killian Roach

What did she say? She asked in an odd way. Something like "Hi, hi. Are you tired of writing prefaces? Are you interested in elisions?" Now, well past when you promised to deliver the essay you are writing in earnest. *Ernest Goes to Jail.* You've thought about elisions, you've spoken to both Ingrids, you have notes. So:

Would she have asked if she knew you don't really like poetry? Apart from Francis Ponge and Eileen Myles, you don't read poetry. You only like it when it's quoted in prose with slashes for line breaks. Maybe the slashes appeal to your preoccupation with reading images as text, making a grammar of images. Why do you dislike poetry? You really just dislike literary criticism, New Criticism in particular. Most guides for literary criticism obscure the interests at work behind literature. No poem is suprahistorical. Over to the bookcase. On a tissue-thin page of your big dictionary the word *elision* is defined, in part, as "the act or instance of dropping out or omitting something: OMISSION, CUT.—of false scenery, explanatory essays, useless subplots."[1] I think elisions are attractive because they lack. This lack, a negative charge, is also a feature of poetry. Poetry lacks but is receptive, and what's received can form super-complex shapes on top of the literal text. These shapes are contingent on and private to the reader, and this receiving animates the text in the present.

Just now, I repaired the fridge in my studio. It wasn't cooling and my milk spoiled and popsicles melted. I found, after staring at the wiring diagram for a very long time, that it needed a new relay. "$9.29." I'm staring at the diagram again now. How would an engineer draw the power flow of a poem? Are the wires the strokes, stems, and swashes of type? Can a word be a switch? Can a line be a transformer? The current is the racing saccade of reading eyes. I think elisions are bus bars, at least in the delicate and unsteady world of this conceit. They are open terminals that pass and ground power. They exist to be provisionally tapped.

I read Frank O'Hara's *Lunch Poems* in the Bridgeport Public Library. I read them because they were there, and I was there because childcare is expensive. What is that phrase about circumstances? We make our own history but not as we please? Sometimes when I'm extremely tired I quietly repeat my circumstances to myself. *My name is. I was born in. I'm the youngest of. I'm going blind because.* This feels comforting but shouldn't be. It's comforting the way meal kits and furnished apartments and dating apps are. It's the pleasure of cession. Is it useful to know I read O'Hara as a tween? Probably not. Is it useful to know that modern poetry was invented and canonized by bigots? Probably yes. What part of that did O'Hara receive? What, in turn, did I? Or did his voice diffuse it?

> It was 3 a.m. of a Saturday night on Fire Island, pitch black on the beach except for the headlights of a disabled taxi and those of another jeep headed its way, sloughing through deep ruts at maybe 25 miles an hour.
>
> Frank O'Hara, one of nine temporarily stranded passengers, stood alone off in the darkness, his companion and friend J.J. Mitchell wasn't sure just where. Within inches of the crippled taxi, the second jeep churned past. Evidently O'Hara was just turning to face a blaze of its lights when it ran him down.[2]

There he was, the passenger of a stalled conveyance, his private machines whirring as he idled nearby, run down like an errant thought. He died the following day, July 24, 1966.

Eliding is a kind of collision, and elisions and contractions are linked. The psychics here are like space weather. Things have their own permeable atmospheres and gravities, and removing or merging anything creates erratic conditions. If you squint, evidence of these forces is perceptible on the things within and nearby. They are dented like car bodies, swollen like embolisms, stretched like elastane, compacted like trash . . . You see these forces only in effect and by impression and must describe them as one makes a cast from a mold or a mold from a cast. An elision makes estranged objects, their binary opposites out of sight. The one constant at work on the weather within an elision is the stream of negatively charged particles blowing through from the original cut—a magnetic solar wind.

Elisions are dangerous. They will support tenuous links between unrelated or uninteresting things. Late last night I fell into the yawning k-hole of an elision. A truly flimsy thought carried me from astrological voids to surface waves, to suction at sea, to the sinking of the replica tall ship *Bounty* during Hurricane Sandy. And then back to the *Bounty*'s role in *The SpongeBob SquarePants Movie* (2004) and *Pirates* (2005), the most expensive porno ever made at the time of its release. I was taught that reading one thing through another should be productive and critical, but there is joy in unfocused work, tenuous links, floppy thoughts . . . Wasting time and attention becomes subversive and generative over time. The pleasure of wandering in an elision is the pleasure of a freedom that's totally personal. There's no need to wonder how your desires and compulsions will affect others.

Anyway, the space of an elision is a hole, not a void, as sculptor Charles Ray has explained.

> The mathematical definition of a hole is an object that you cannot shrink to point topologically. . . . You cannot shrink a hole to a point. It becomes an armature. It becomes like a seed of a sculpture. All sculptures have armatures, whether that armature is a thought or an idea—all ideas have armatures. An armature can be kind of like a wire in the brain that you still start building around, putting things, holding things onto.[3]

The idea of a hole as armature essentially describes the form of a Lee Bontecou wall-mounted sculpture. Ray knows this and acknowledges it indirectly at the end of his lecture. Hers are the first sculptures that incorporate armature as a formal element. You clearly see their construction and her fastidious labor. Her hundred welds and hundreds of copper wire sutures make intricate, electric webs of activity that describe and form holes. Each sculpture is a "grotesque and sinister machine the use for which escapes you, though it obviously exists."[4] Bontecou is it, the model, my model, and my last bulleted note. Any one of her artworks would make a better explanatory essay than this one.

NOTES

1. *Webster's Third New International Dictionary, Unabridged* (Springfield, MA: Merriam-Webster, 2002), under "elision."

2. Peter Schjeldahl, "Frank O'Hara: He Made Things and People Sacred," *Village Voice*, August 11, 1966, 11–12.

3. Charles Ray, "Thoughts on Sculpture," lecture, The Menil Collection, Houston, October 23, 2015.

4. John Ashbery, "Fire That Burns in the Heart of the Void," *New York Herald Tribune*, April 20, 1965, 5.

Iteration IV

April 27–June 20, 2023

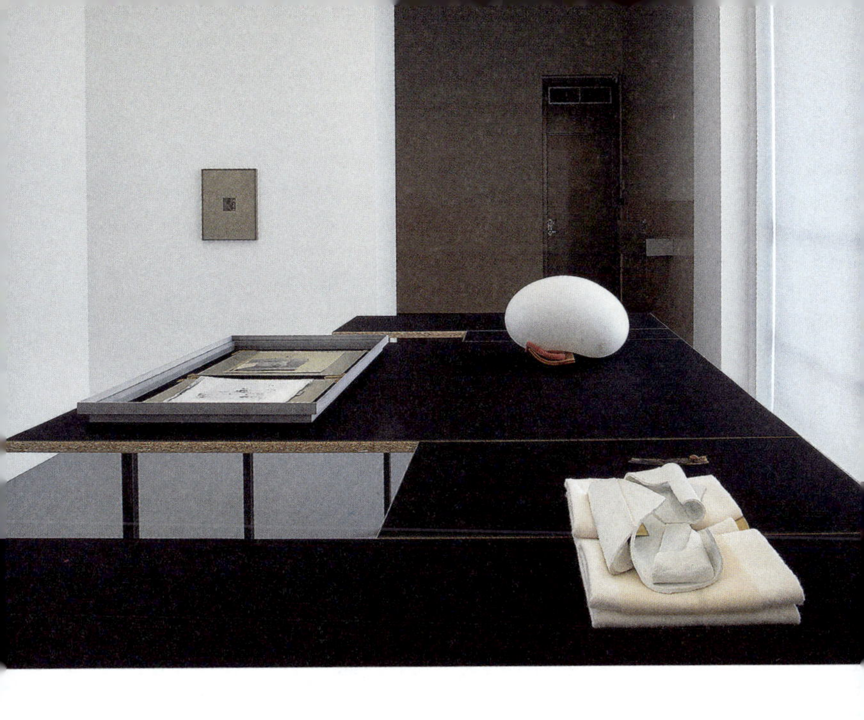

Umbra (Etui 03), 2021

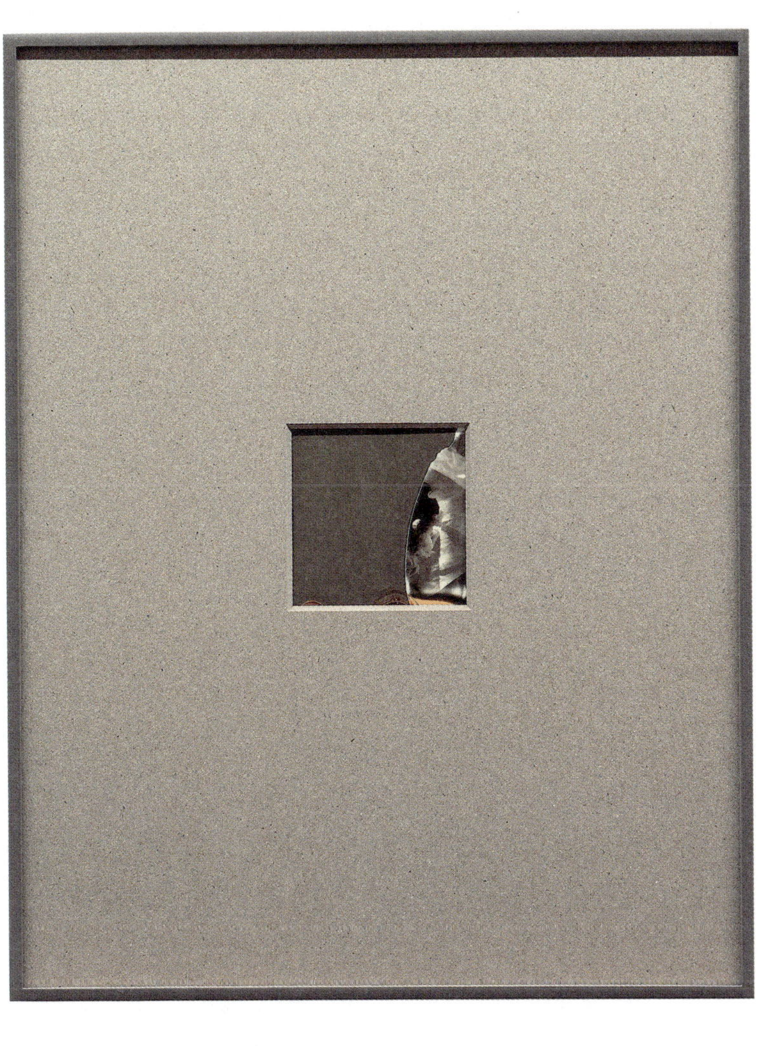

Subject Position, 2022–23

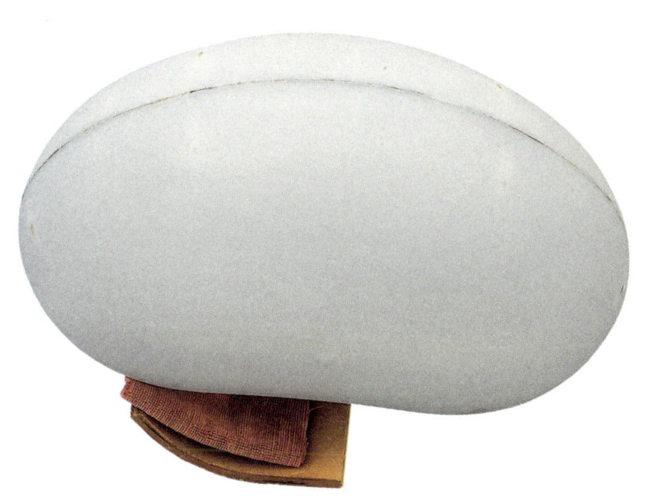

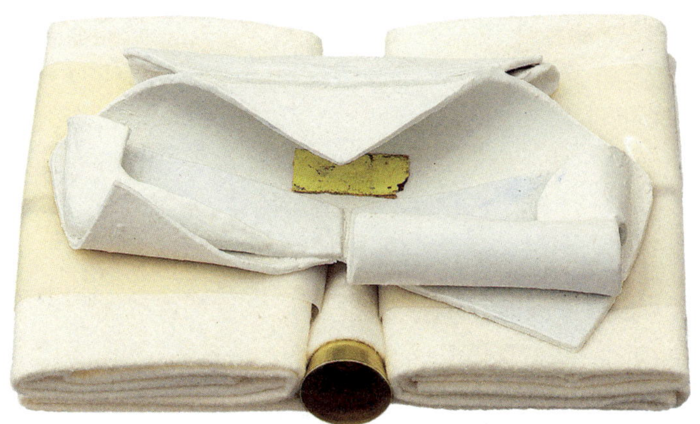

Clock / Painting, 2023

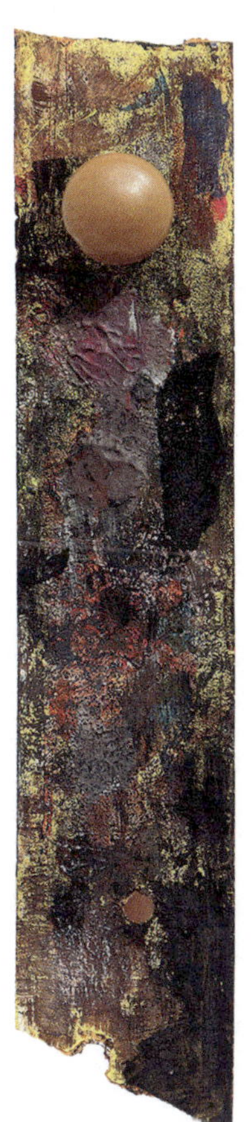

Artists Book (detail), 2010–23

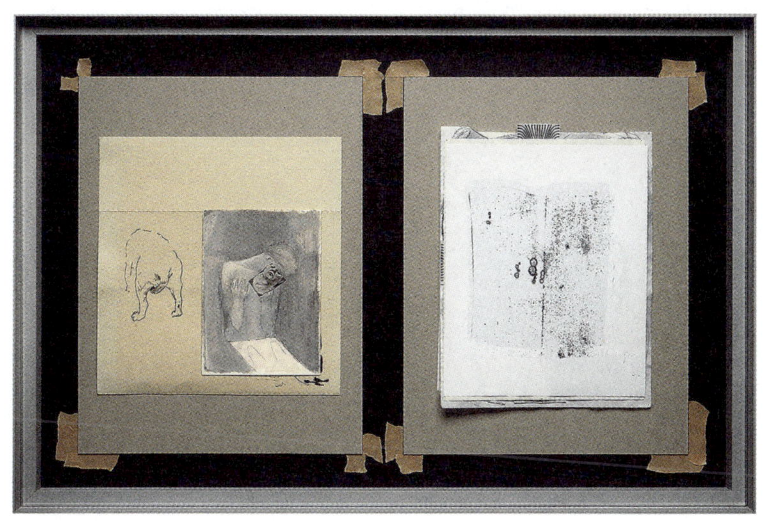

Introductions by Kate Zambreno (replica), 2018/2023

HEAD, HOUSE, LIGHT

Can a text be a house. Can a paragraph be a room. Can a sentence be a window. Wittgenstein's sister, Gretl, thought helping to design her large city house in Vienna would be a good activity for her brother, the philosopher. Wittgenstein was still recovering from the war, and, he thought, philosophy. He was working as an assistant gardener at a monastery outside of the city, and was mulling one of two possibilities for the future: either becoming a monk or committing suicide. He was in a form of exile, owing to what has been referred to as the Haidbauer incident, when working as an elementary schoolteacher at a village school in rural Austria, he hit an 11-year-old boy, one Josef Haidbauer, so hard on the head during class that the boy collapsed unconscious. There was a hearing, in which the judge requested a psychiatric examination—Wittgenstein fled, although he returned a decade later to apologize to the students, who were now older. Except for hitting the slower students, Wittgenstein was a wonderful teacher: he designed buildings and steamships with them, dissected animals, took long treks in the woods and identified plants, took the train to Vienna and discussed the various architecture of the buildings there. Even though he was a steel heir, he had given his fortune away, and slept in the kitchen, eating only oatmeal out of a pot he never cleaned. Of course, his family was concerned. There is a letter from his brother Paul, the one-armed pianist, to one of Wittgenstein's friends, worried that his brother was not eating correctly for his colitis. He was supposed to only assist the architect, who had studied under Adolf Loos, on the design of the house, one of those cold modernist constructions of three white cubes. He was put in charge of the interiors: windows, doors, doorknobs, and radiators. As befitting the fastidious philosopher who once studied aeronautical engineering, he became absorbed in the project and completely took over, even moving into the small architect's office to live there full-time. He had to design the door handles himself, which took him a year. The heights for the door handles were minutely designed according to door type. It took another year to design the radiators. Each of the large vertical windows was covered with a metal screen, moved by a pulley system Wittgenstein designed. He insisted that everything be designed according to exact proportions—including having the ceiling raised by 30 millimeters. He even wanted to make his own version of a head that he had disliked in one of the sculptures that were commissioned for the entrance way—his sister placed the plaster cast of the head he designed in the house. Of course, upon its completion, she didn't want to live there, and eventually the house was sold to the Bulgarian embassy. After finishing the house three years later, he returned to Cambridge and philosophy, wanting to work now on visual space. In his later *Philosophical Investigations,* he imagined thought as taking place in a room. "A person caught in a philosophical confusion is like a man in a room who wants to get out but doesn't know how." Wittgenstein himself liked to think in Spartan surroundings—sometimes a chair in a room was all that he needed.

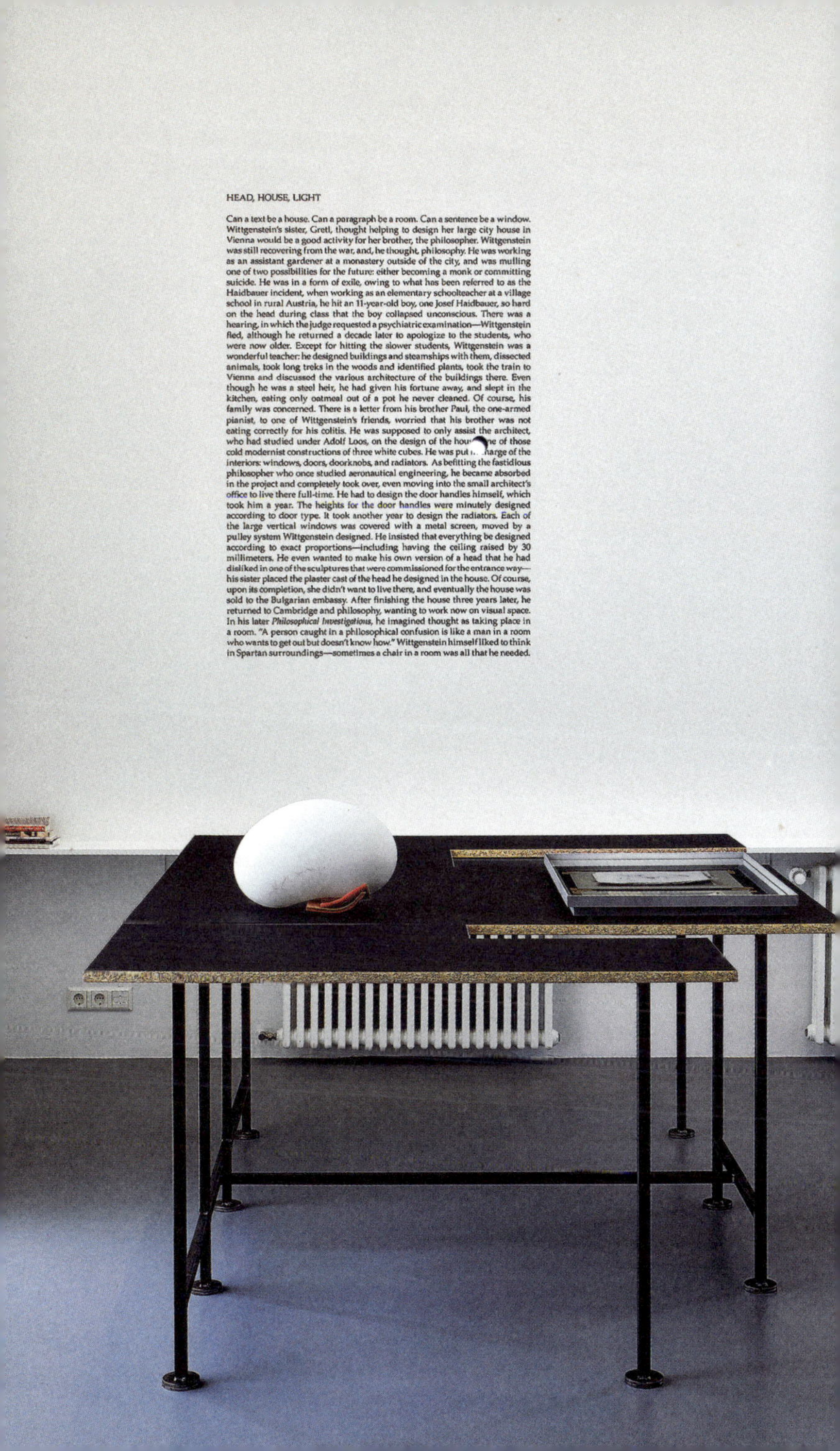
HEAD, HOUSE, LIGHT
Can a text be a house. Can a paragraph be a room. Can a sentence be a window. Wittgenstein's sister, Gretl, thought helping to design her large city house in Vienna would be a good activity for her brother, the philosopher. Wittgenstein was still recovering from the war, and, he thought, philosophy. He was working as an assistant gardener at a monastery outside of the city, and was mulling one of two possibilities for the future: either becoming a monk or committing suicide. He was in a form of exile, owing to what has been referred to as the Haidbauer incident, when working as an elementary schoolteacher at a village school in rural Austria, he hit an 11-year-old boy, one Josef Haidbauer, so hard on the head during class that the boy collapsed unconscious. There was a hearing, in which the judge requested a psychiatric examination—Wittgenstein fled, although he returned a decade later to apologize to the students, who were now older. Except for hitting the slower students, Wittgenstein was a wonderful teacher: he designed buildings and steamships with them, dissected animals, took long treks in the woods and identified plants, took the train to Vienna and discussed the various architecture of the buildings there. Even though he was a steel heir, he had given his fortune away, and slept in the kitchen, eating only oatmeal out of a pot he never cleaned. Of course, his family was concerned. There is a letter from his brother Paul, the one-armed pianist, to one of Wittgenstein's friends, worried that his brother was not eating correctly for his colitis. He was supposed to only assist the architect, who had studied under Adolf Loos, on the design of the hou… ne of those cold modernist constructions of three white cubes. He was put … harge of the interiors: windows, doors, doorknobs, and radiators. As befitting the fastidious philosopher who once studied aeronautical engineering, he became absorbed in the project and completely took over, even moving into the small architect's office to live there full-time. He had to design the door handles himself, which took him a year. The heights for the door handles were minutely designed according to door type. It took another year to design the radiators. Each of the large vertical windows was covered with a metal screen, moved by a pulley system Wittgenstein designed. He insisted that everything be designed according to exact proportions—including having the ceiling raised by 30 millimeters. He even wanted to make his own version of a head that he had disliked in one of the sculptures that were commissioned for the entrance way—his sister placed the plaster cast of the head he designed in the house. Of course, upon its completion, she didn't want to live there, and eventually the house was sold to the Bulgarian embassy. After finishing the house three years later, he returned to Cambridge and philosophy, wanting to work now on visual space. In his later *Philosophical Investigations*, he imagined thought as taking place in a room. "A person caught in a philosophical confusion is like a man in a room who wants to get out but doesn't know how." Wittgenstein himself liked to think in Spartan surroundings—sometimes a chair in a room was all that he needed.

uildings there.

way, and slept i

eaned. Of cours

Paul, the one-a

his brother wa

y assist the arch

e hous[illegible]ne of

as put i[illegible]harge

efitting the fasti

, he became abs

o the small arch

A small bore of light, but did it see her, 2023

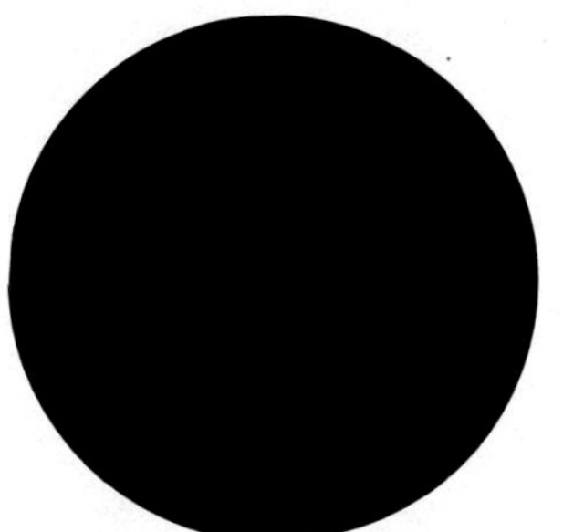

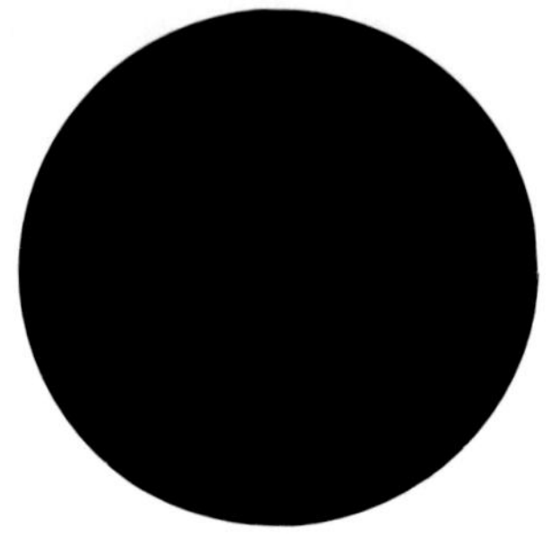

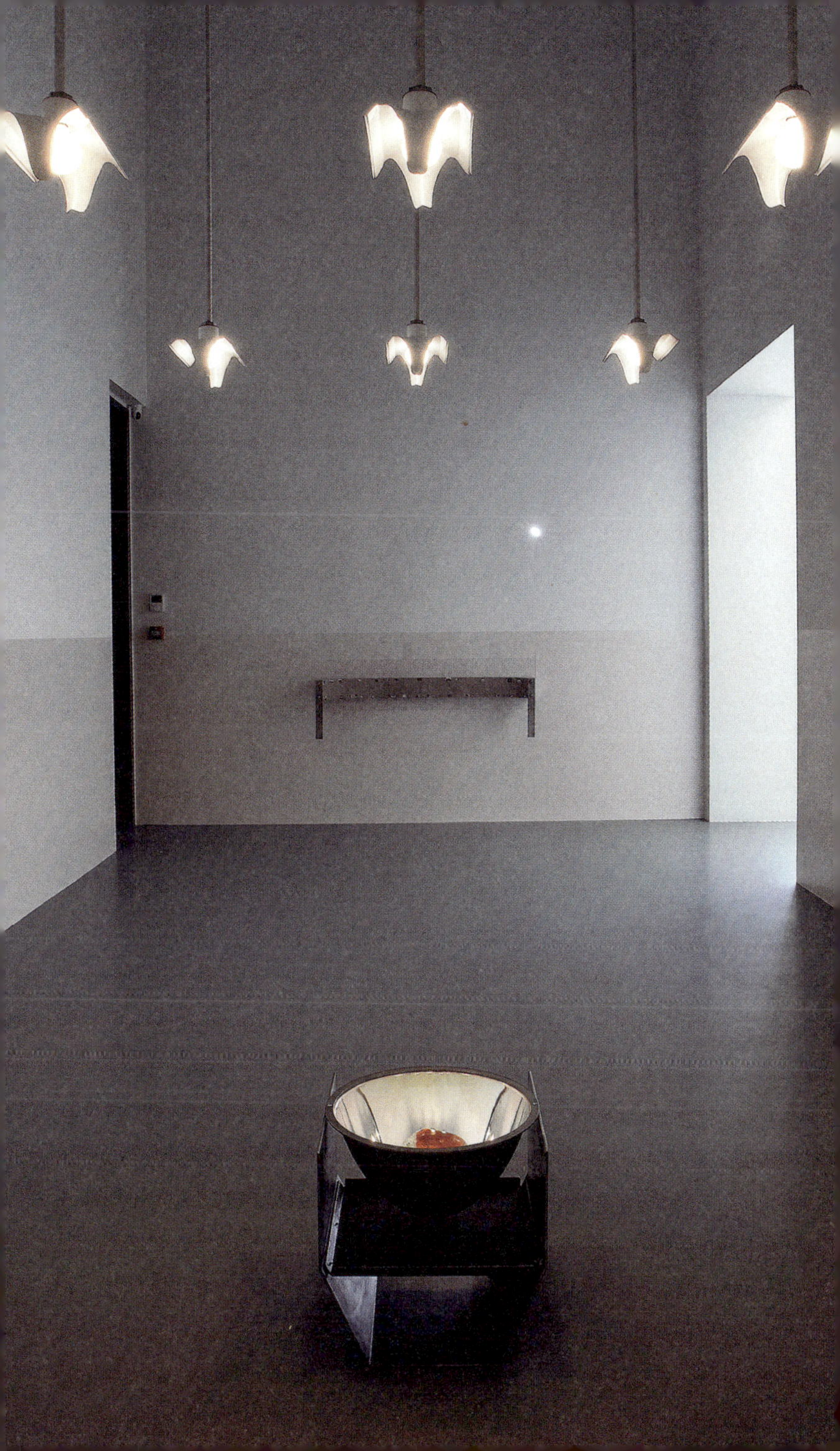

Plen, cycle, 2022–23

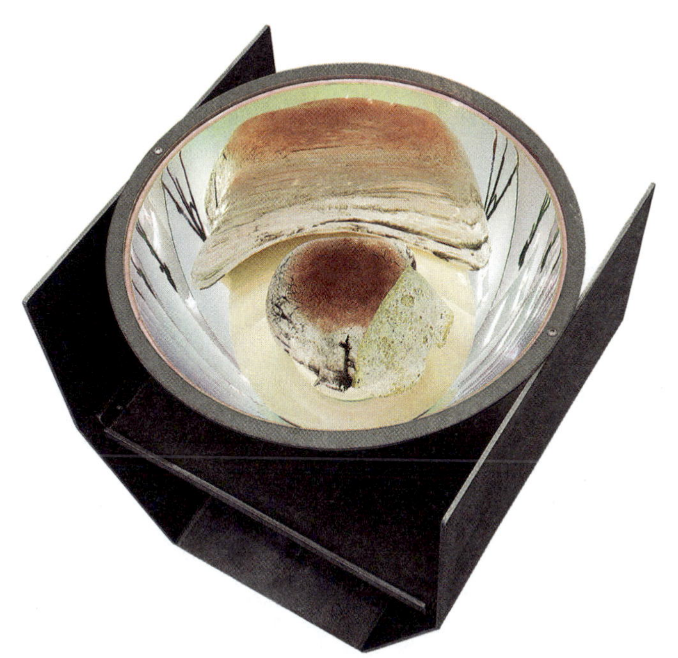

Camera (am I disorganized because I lost something I didn't need?), 2020–22

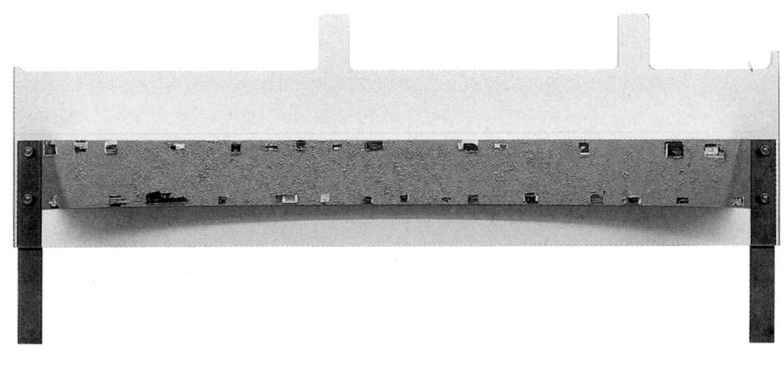

May 30–June 12

Artists Book (detail), 2010–23

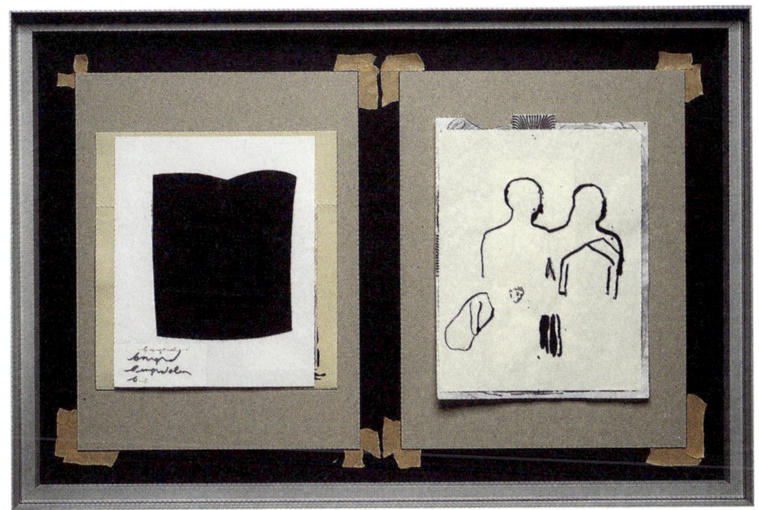

June 13–20

Artists Book (detail), 2010–23

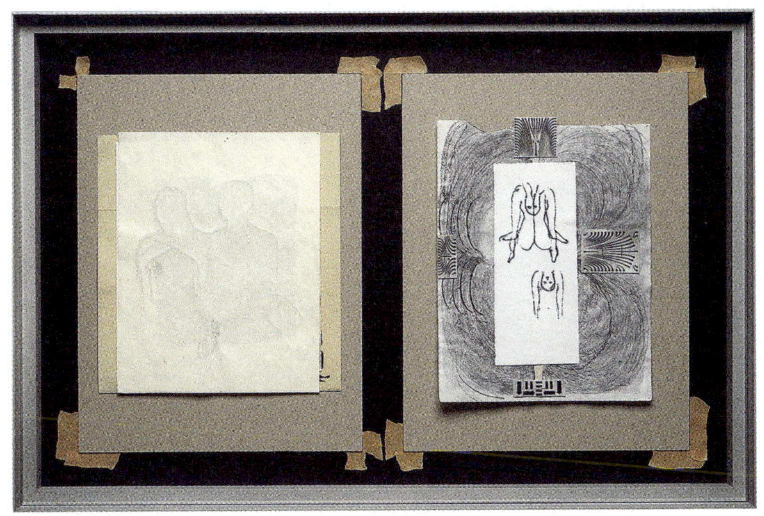

EXCERPT FROM *FOURTH PERSON SINGULAR*

Nuar Alsadir

On the local platform at 86th Street waiting for a 6 Train, I noticed written on a column in thick Sharpie, "Fuck Lyric":

FUCK LYRIC

I felt stunned, stood staring so long at those two words I almost missed the train that briefly opened its light to me. Of course, I thought later, it's possible there's some asshole named Lyric somewhere in New York City who needs to fuck off. But the message, as I took it, resonates with a struggle I've had for years with poetics, the figure of address, and larger questions of selfhood.

It all began in a barn in Provincetown. I was grappling with the recognition that even though I'd developed an aversion to confessional poetry, the poems I found moving, which served as my measure of a poem's value, were invariably lyric, written in the first person and addressed—as is all speech—to a second person, whether circumscribed or implied, a *you* without whom the poem wouldn't, or, perhaps couldn't, have been written. There I was, off-season, at land's edge, in a world populated by Portuguese fishermen and an erasing darkness that set in by mid-afternoon. There I was, but where were *you*?

I am never merely writing, but always writing *to you*. In response to a college friend's praise of her letters, Marianne Moore responded, "My letters are better than my stories I suppose because I am not self-conscious. Because I am thinking of '*you*' (~~whoever you are~~)." The *you* of any letter is inevitably multiple, at once the letter's explicit addressee, an unknown *you* "(whoever you are)," but also the unknown you struck-out "(~~whoever you are~~)," which may be a shift back to a known you or another shift away. *You* become a position figures pass through, momentarily occupy:

Marcet

you

whoever you are

(~~whoever you are~~)

But if *you* are an endless chain of metonymic displacements, then what am *I*, that self that organizes around thinking of *you*? And why is it that writing a lyric poem that has an *I* that matches up with the person I consider myself to be in my everyday life induces shame? How can the *I* of a poem—also a chain of metonymic displacements—maintain the same multiplicity as *you*, resist adopting a fiction of a singular voice, have the intimate quality of a notebook without the intimate content, become the position or mouthpiece through which the world, rather than an individual, speaks?

> Yukel, you have never been at ease in your own skin. You have never been here, but always elsewhere, ahead of yourself or behind like winter in the eyes of autumn or summer in the eyes of spring, in the past or in the future like those syllables whose passage from night to day is so much like lightning that it merges with the movement of the pen.

The writer who has at no point belonged anywhere, who like Edmond Jabès's Yukel, has never been at ease in his own skin, lives life in the "elsewhere," a province of exile, a region reached through the movement of the pen that collapses winter with autumn, summer with spring, past with future, night with day—but also the embodied self with concurrent selves in alternate space-times. The one who speaks "I" becomes a many who speaks "I" or "he" while meaning "I" and "he," but also "you," "we" and "they." My attempt to make sense of this voice that speaks as one but out of the many—first, second and third person simultaneously—led nowhere, into the nowhere of the mind, which is also an elsewhere, and, like the unconscious, a space of possibility.

And so it arrived that way, as a fragment in the voice of dream, "The fourth person singular exists in the fourth dimension."

Yet how does one decipher here into logic what was already known, but only elsewhere—ahead, behind and out of skin?

"There are things we've never seen, heard or even felt," wrote Kafka in a letter, "and we can't prove they exist, though no one has yet tried, but we run after them, without knowing which direction to run in, and we catch up with them without reaching them, and, still complete with clothes, family souvenirs and social relationships, we fall into them as into a grave that was only a shadow on the road." The runners Kafka refers to in this passage—running after "things" they have "never seen, heard or even felt," things they "can't prove ... exist"—make up a "we," but also a "no one," having not "yet tried" to prove the existence of the perceived "things." This trial exists in the future, a future containing the things we will run after but "catch up with ... without reaching"—the Real we search for but never find—because we live in the shadow of things, even a grave, fall even into the shadow of our own death, which is the point of certainty toward which every being is supposedly running. A runner of the we, who is also no one, exits the world of proof and enters a shadow region, a region whose fourth dimension has an elsewhere that relegates us to a space-time in which we will always "catch up ... without reaching."

Four-dimensional space-time takes into account three dimensions of space and a fourth dimension of time. A point (P) existing at a particular location in space at a particular time is called an "event." Before Einstein's theory of special relativity, time and space were thought to be absolute: absolute time was thought to exist independently of space, absolute space thought to have a physical reality

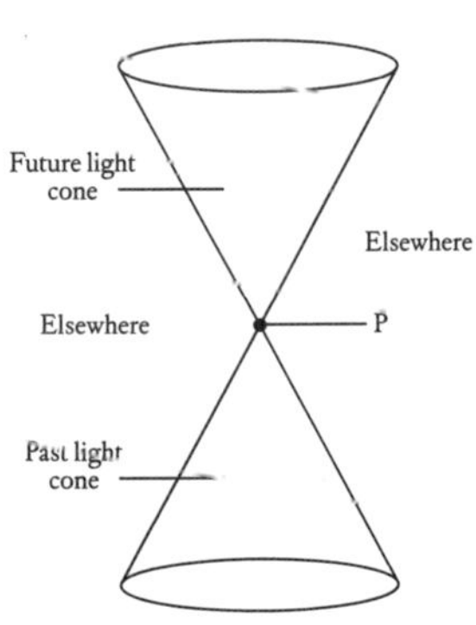

independent of any object. Einstein demonstrated that objects, rather than existing in space, are spatially extended, which makes the concept of "empty space" impossible. If you transpose his theory to time, "now" also loses its meaning as an absolute because a specific event exists only in the context of a specific frame of reference. If a self were thought of within this context of four dimensions, there would also be no absolute self or identity (I). Similarly spatially extended, (I) would exist within but also beyond, out of, skin.

In the diagram above, originally presented by Stephen Hawking, a specific event is termed (P). All events that can be affected by what happens at (P) by particle or waves traveling at or below the speed of light are in or on the future light cone of (P), while all events that can affect (P) by a particle or wave traveling at or below the speed of light are in the past light cone of (P). All other events are in the elsewhere of (P), where they have no effect on and are not affected by what happens at (P). If the sun ceased to shine, Hawking proposes, because the sun is in our elsewhere and light takes eight minutes to travel from the sun into our future light cone, events on earth would be affected only after an eight-minute lag.

This lag, in relation to an individual, would perhaps represent happenings in the elsewhere of our psychic structure that we do not feel the effects of simultaneous to their occurrence, similar to what, in psychoanalytic temporality, is described by Freud as *Nachträglichkeit*, translated by Lacan as *après-coup* and later put into English by Jean Laplanche as *afterwardness. Nachträglichkeit* describes another kind of lag, in which what is experienced by a person in the present has already happened in the past, but in a form that they weren't able to assimilate into meaning and therefore, rather than registering consciously, left unconscious psychical traces. [Donald] Winnicott

This compulsive search in the future for something from the past can take the form of writing. Gerard Manley Hopkins: "my lament/ Is cries countless, cries like dead letters sent/ To dearest him that lives alas! away."

describes a similar dynamic in which a person fears finding a "detail" from the past that is, ironically, "compulsively looked for in the future." The lag here is in the registration of an event in consciousness rather than in space-time. When the unconscious, which remains for the most part in the elsewhere, makes its way into our past light cone—affecting (P) and (I) in the present—or makes its way into our future light cone—affecting (P) and (I) in the future—it becomes conscious, but in a form that is altered due to a variation in vantage point. We are always operating with this lag to a degree, even neurologically, as what we experience as now is, in fact, about eight milliseconds in the past, as that is the time it takes the brain to process and put together data into a conscious representation. There is, in other words, no present—and time isn't linear. The past and the future do not merely affect the present, but represent themselves as separate subjects that cannot be easily assimilated into our understanding of a particular moment.

When the woman from the past asks the protagonist of Chris Marker's *La Jetée* about his necklace—"the combat necklace he wore at the start of the war that is to break our some day"— he "invents an explanation."

Being moved to write lyric poetry is a kind of compulsion to invent explanations as a way of searching for and attempting to master what you fear finding that has already been experienced, an unthought known or a known that has been thought by a version of self that is yet to come, that is confined to catching up without reaching.

By the time our perception of ourselves registers, we have already moved on (however slightly) from that particular self and are looking back from a distance (however miniscule), so that the perceived *I* has become a *not-I*. This outside perspective on oneself can provide a basis for shame, which involves looking back at the self through the eyes of another. It also

Years ago, reading André Breton's *Mad Love*, I was struck by the line, "One must alway live as if on the brink of love!" I carried it around as precept, but when I turned back to the book to refind the sentence, it wasn't there. I'm certain Breton wrote it, but, at this point (P), Breton and the past self that was moved by Breton are equally separate subjects that have traveled out of my past light cone and into my Elsewhere—

makes of the surrounding selves, in the past and future light cones, neighbor selves, who should indeed be loved, but as *whom*? (Lacan points out that most people hate themselves.)

We superimpose ourselves onto others each time we address them, which is another way our neighbors become other kinds of self. When we construct any form of speech that we plan to address to another, there's a split second in which we exit our own position and imaginatively project ourselves into the position of the other person to envision their response to what we plan to say, and then quickly edit our speech to accommodate that imagined reception. [Mikhail] Bakhtin calls this dynamic *addressivity*: our dialogue is, at first, always internal, a communication between the self and a psychic representation of another person. We do a sort of test drive in our minds on our imagined representation of the other before taking our speech into the world and addressing it to the living, thinking, feeling person before us.

The irony here is that it is our own mind projectively externalized that makes us cower, a mind we imaginatively create for the other that can never match up with the contents of their actual mind. Lyric address, then, occurs not only between an I and a you, but between separate parts of mind and different states of self. We use our expectations of how people (or versions of ourselves) we've known well have responded in the past as an index when anticipating how the person before us will respond in the present. Freud called this dynamic transference—we transfer our expectations and feelings about known figures onto someone in the moment

What is your aim in philosophy?—To show the fly the way out of the fly-bottle.

"Beyond being, is a Third person who is not defined by selfhood."

in order to figure them out—which is, in a sense, *Nachträglichkeit* inverted, the past resignifying the future as opposed to the past being given meaning retroactively. He believed that analyzing the transference was the key to a psychoanalytic cure: it helps people develop the ability to be conscious of what is happening in the moment, as well as what had traveled from the elsewhere to affect it, so that they have the opportunity to make choices about how to behave in the present rather than acting on a kind of autopilot. Psychoanalysis is, therefore, also lyric, involves an I addressing a thou, a patient addressing an analyst, a present self addressing a past self, a past self addressing a present self, an address from an imagined mind (as with addressivity) or a message transmitted to or from a Third, now in our elsewhere, which will only register later, afterwards, if we can catch up and reach it.

Who is the third who walks always beside you?
When I count, there are only you and I together
But when I look ahead up the white road
There is always another one walking beside you
Gliding wrapt in a brown mantle, hooded
I do not know whether a man or a woman
—But who is that on the other side of you?

Four-dimensional space-time is always relational, and to speak about the absolute past and absolute future in light cones is to have always already chosen a fixed observer. Moore lived with her mother until she died. Her mother was, in many ways, an inhibiting force Moore had to get away from early in her career in order to write. Moore, yearning to be part of a literary community, wrote, early in her career, poems addressed to literary figures she admired—"To Bernard Shaw: A Prize Bird," "To Browning." Those early lyric poems are filled with emotion—in fact, "To Browning" is based on love letters between Robert Browning and Elizabeth Barrett Browning in which they discuss a yellow rose, infidelity, their passion. In Moore's poem, she steps into their circuit of communication—not quite as Browning, but to the side of him, to enter their discussion and then to address a version of

Browning himself. These early poems, essentially odes, are (for her) quite charged.

When her first book, *Selected Poems*, was published, however, she replaced each title that had addressed a poem to a specific figure with an impersonal title—"To Robert Browning" became "Injudicious Gardening," for example—and addressed the entire collection to her mother in a postscript at the end of the book. In redressing the address, particularly in addressing the poems to an inhibiting figure, the emotion in the poems—even as the poems were essentially the same beyond their tides—escaped.

Dedications imply giving, and we do not care to make a gift of what is insufficient; but in my immediate family there is one "who thinks in a particular way"; and I should like to add that where there is an effect of thought or pith in these pages, the thinking and often the actual phrases are hers.

A circuit of communication plays into the construction of any utterance and involves our past selves, figures from our past that communicate unconsciously with us and have shaped our expectations, the person before us whose reception of our speech we anticipate and restructure around, the voices and objects in our external and internal worlds. Any utterance is a record of the four-dimensional space-time surrounding a moment—the (I), the past and future light cones, everything in the elsewhere and the lag created as something in the elsewhere move towards our future or out of our past light cones—a period during which we experience psychical traces of things we may perceive but cannot know. Perhaps Moore was "not self-conscious" when "thinking of *you* (~~whoever you are~~)" because her addressee occupied a position that Bakhtin terms a *superaddressee*,

My dear, accept this dedication; it is given over, as it were, blindfolded, but therefore undisturbed by any consideration, in sincerity. Who you are, I know not; where you are, I know not; what your name is, I know not. Yet you are my hope, my pride, and my unknown honor.

a "(third), whose absolutely just understanding is presumed," or what Michael Warner calls an "indefinite strange[r]," a figure that allows you to speak into a "social imaginary," an "environment of strangerhood [that] is the necessary premise of some of our most prized ways of being." Only to this *you* can one speak as (I), in the fourth person singular. You are the indefinite stranger. Can you hear me? I'm writing from elsewhere. This book is for *you* (~~whoever you are~~).

Iteration V

June 21–July 31, 2023

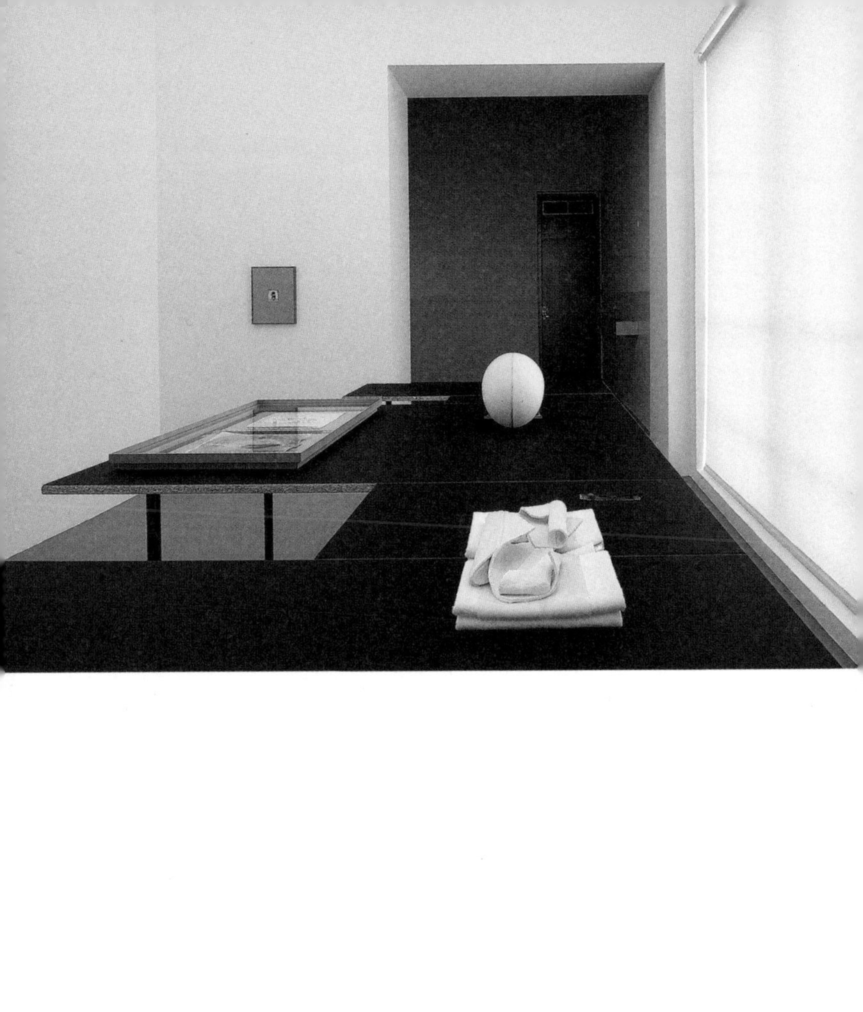

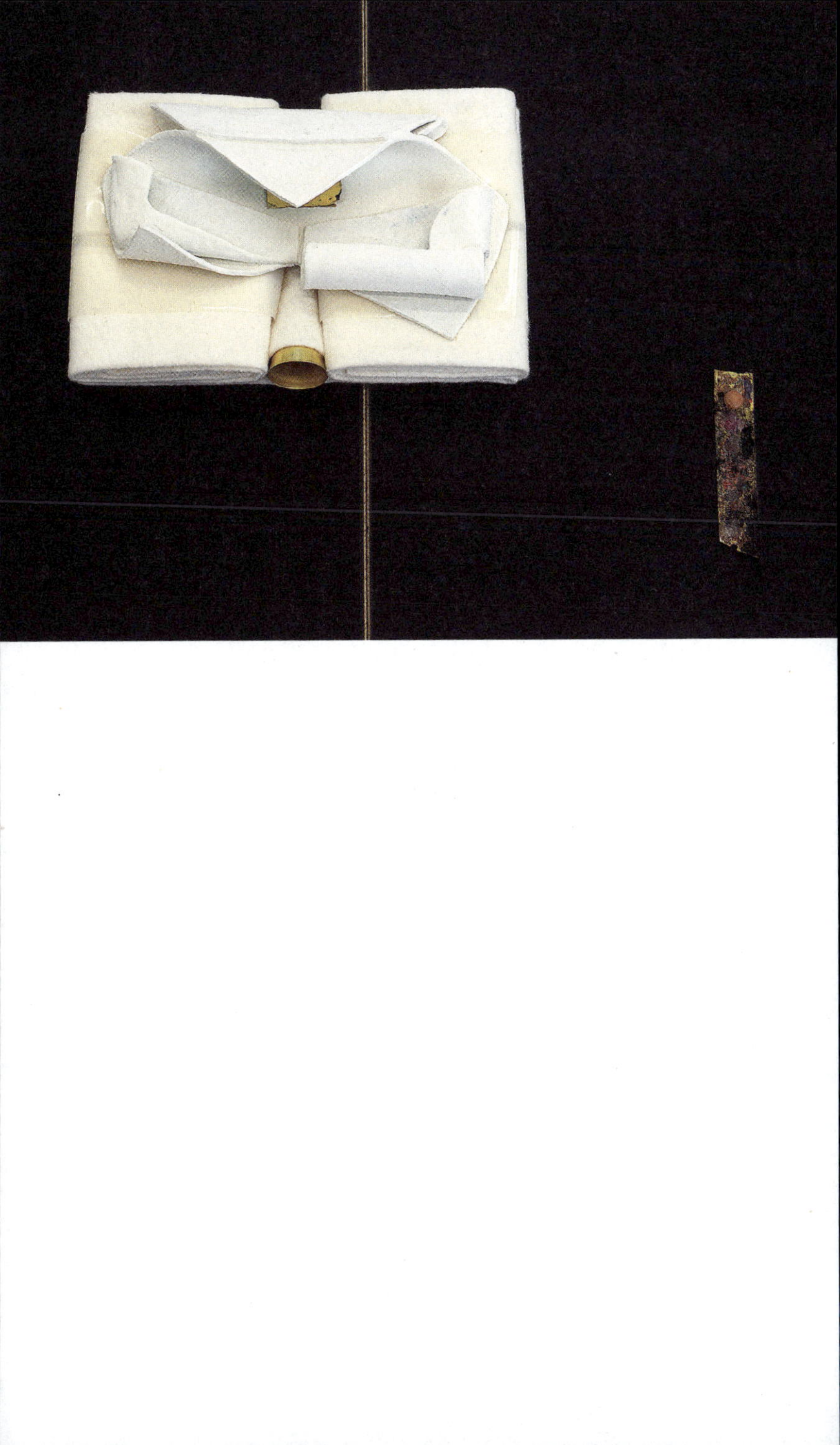

HEAD, HOUSE, LIGHT

Can a text be a house. Can a paragraph be a room. Can a sentence be a window. Wittgenstein's sister, Gretl, thought helping to design her large city house in Vienna would be a good activity for her brother, the philosopher. Wittgenstein was still recovering from the war, and, he thought, philosophy. He was working as an assistant gardener at a monastery outside of the city, and was mulling one of two possibilities for the future: either becoming a monk or committing suicide. He was in a form of exile, owing to what has been referred to as the Haidbauer incident, when working as an elementary schoolteacher at a village school in rural Austria, he hit an 11-year-old boy, one Josef Haidbauer, so hard on the head during class that the boy collapsed unconscious. There was a hearing, in which the judge requested a psychiatric examination—Wittgenstein fled, although he returned a decade later to apologize to the students, who were now older. Except for hitting the slower students, Wittgenstein was a wonderful teacher: he designed buildings and steamships with them, dissected animals, took long treks in the woods and identified plants, took the train to Vienna and discussed the various architecture of the buildings there. Even though he was a steel heir, he had given his fortune away, and slept in the kitchen, eating only oatmeal out of a pot he never cleaned. Of course, his family was concerned. There is a letter from his brother Paul, the one-armed pianist, to one of Wittgenstein's friends, worried that his brother was not eating correctly for his colitis. He was supposed to only assist the architect, who had studied under Adolf Loos, on the design of the ho [illegible] e of those cold modernist constructions of three white cubes. He was pu [illegible] arge of the interiors: windows, doors, doorknobs, and radiators. As befitting the fastidious philosopher who once studied aeronautical engineering, he became absorbed in the project and completely took over, even moving into the small architect's office to live there full-time. He had to design the door handles himself, which took him a year. The heights for the door handles were minutely designed according to door type. It took another year to design the radiators. Each of the large vertical windows was covered with a metal screen, moved by a pulley system Wittgenstein designed. He insisted that everything be designed according to exact proportions—including having the ceiling raised by 30 millimeters. He even wanted to make his own version of a head that he had disliked in one of the sculptures that were commissioned for the entrance way—his sister placed the plaster cast of the head he designed in the house. Of course, upon its completion, she didn't want to live there, and eventually the house was sold to the Bulgarian embassy. After finishing the house three years later, he returned to Cambridge and philosophy, wanting to work now on visual space. In his later *Philosophical Investigations*, he imagined thought as taking place in a room. "A person caught in a philosophical confusion is like a man in a room who wants to get out but doesn't know how." Wittgenstein himself liked to think in Spartan surroundings—sometimes a chair in a room was all that he needed.

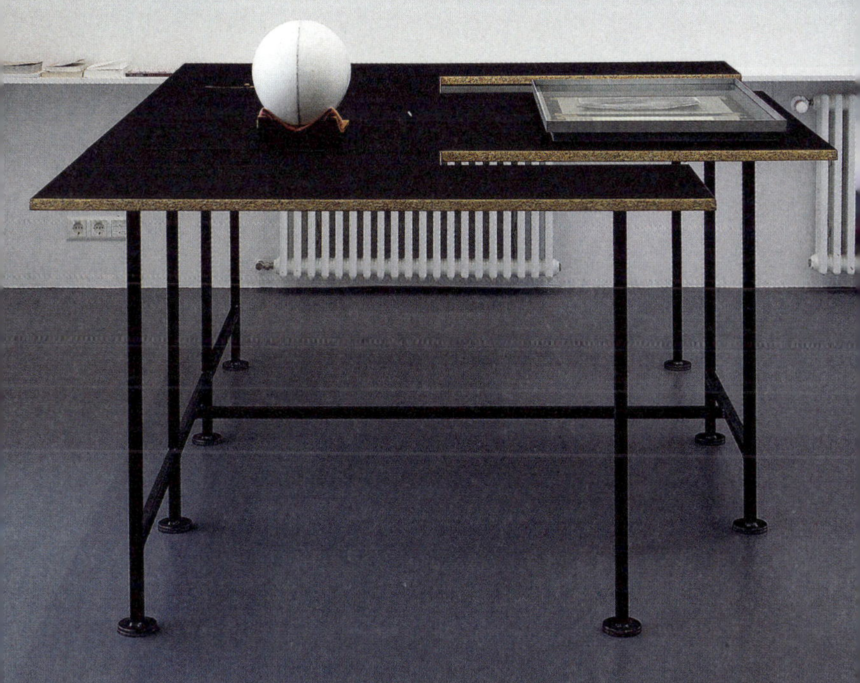

Subject Position, 2022–23

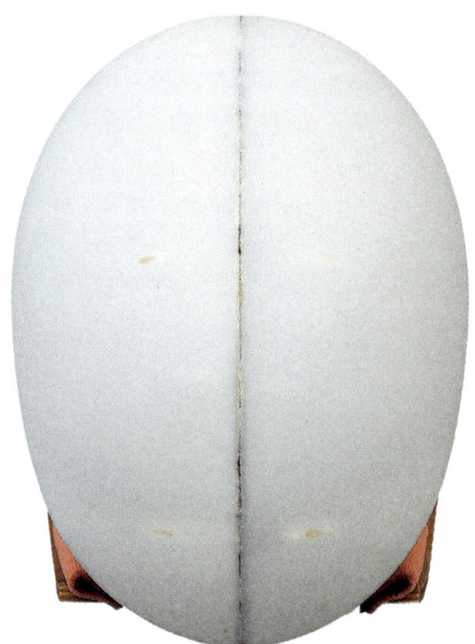

Artists Book (detail), 2010–23

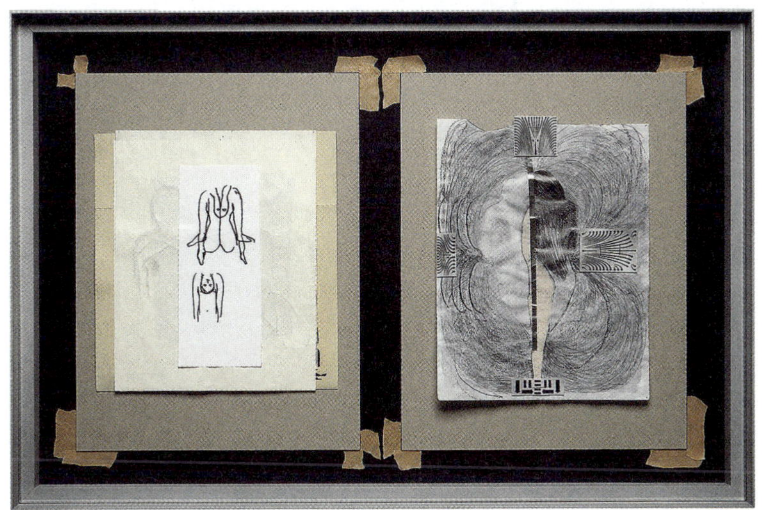

Umbra (Back of Head 01), 2021

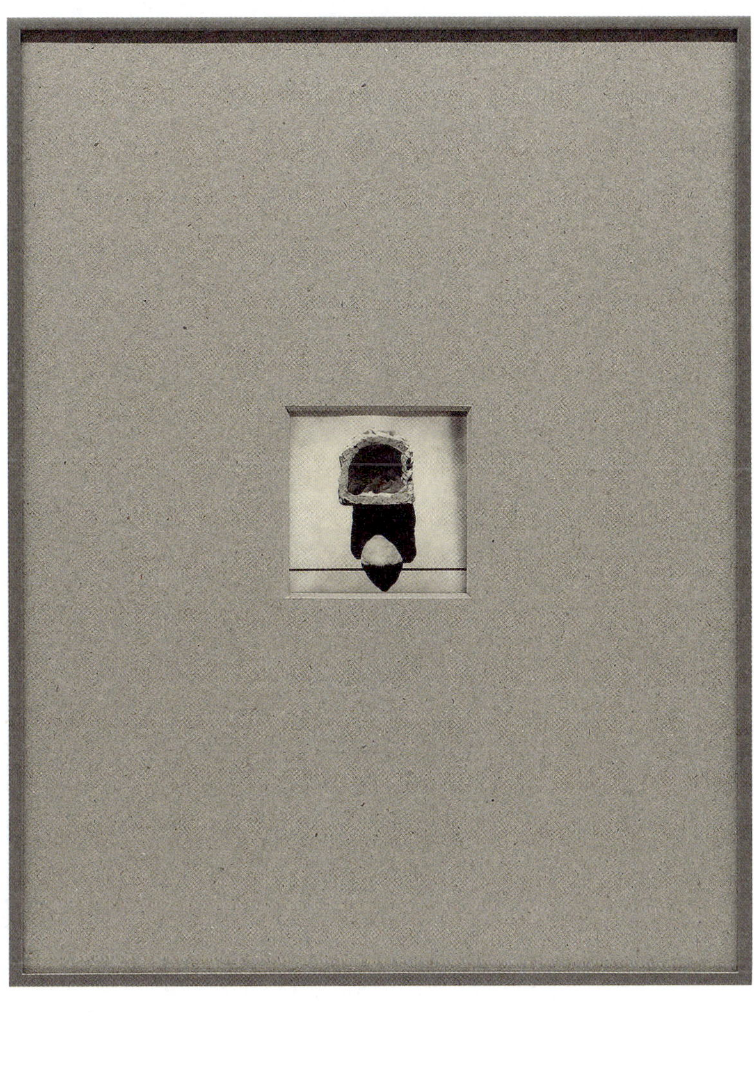

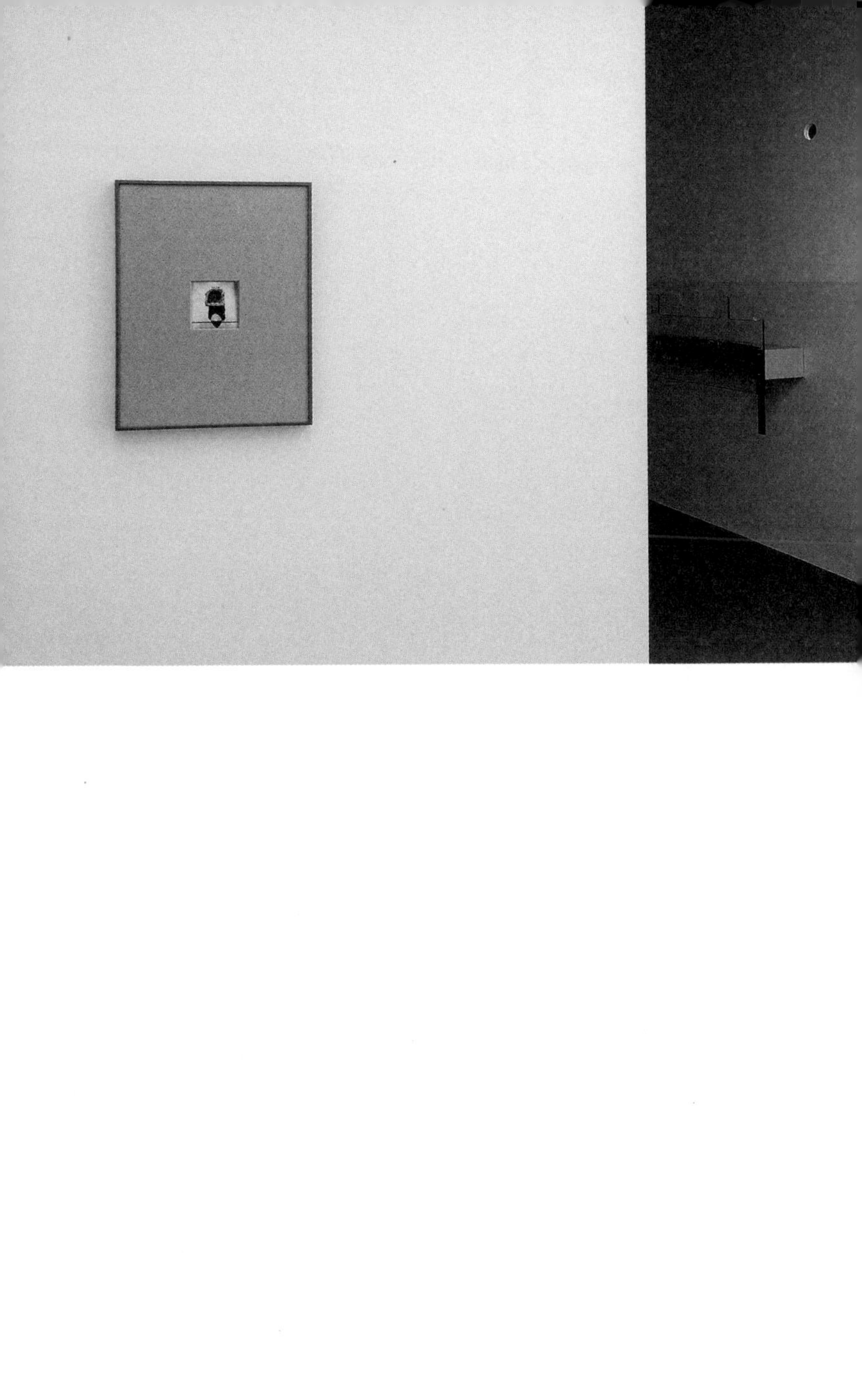

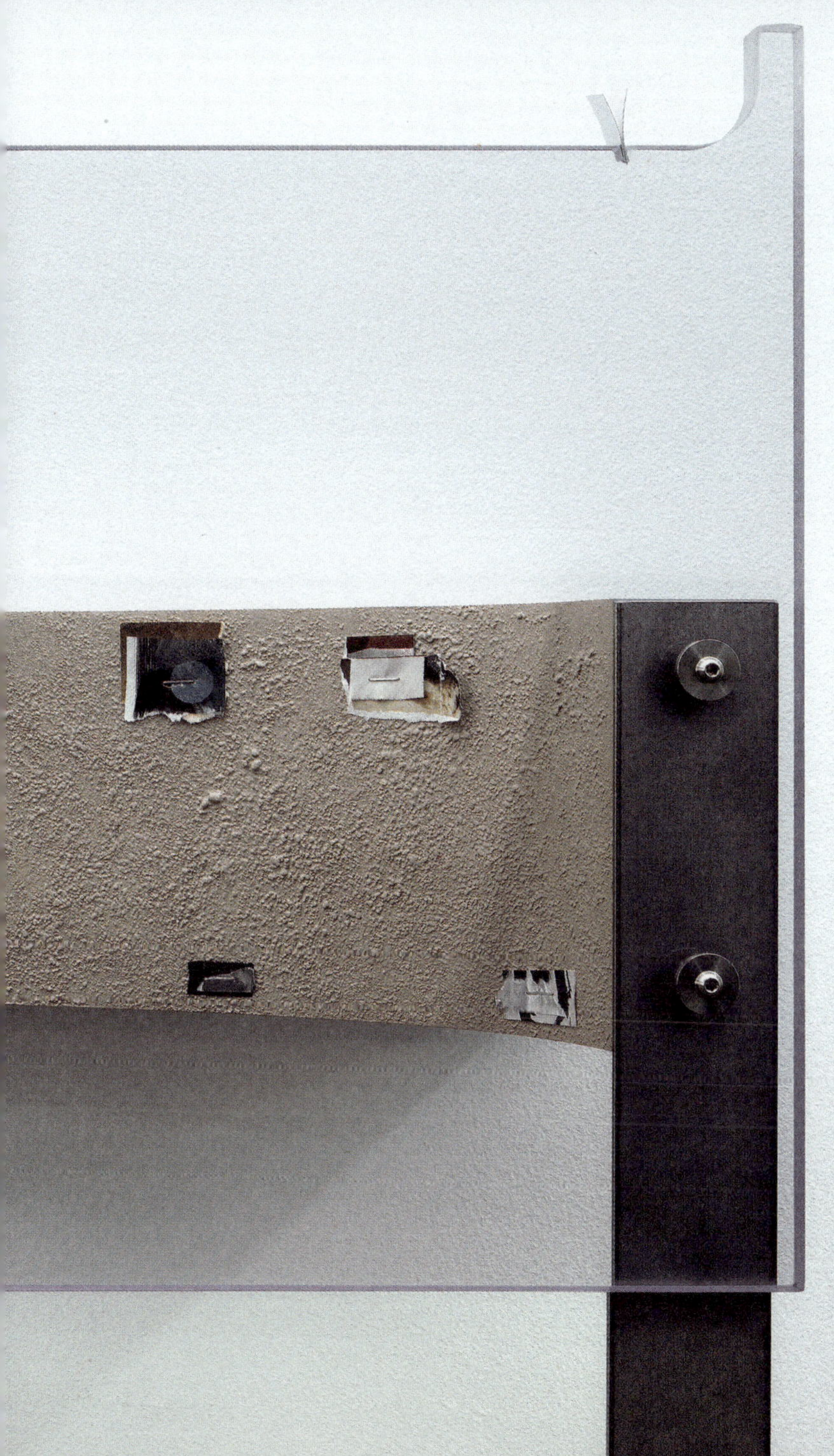

Plen, cycle, 2022–23

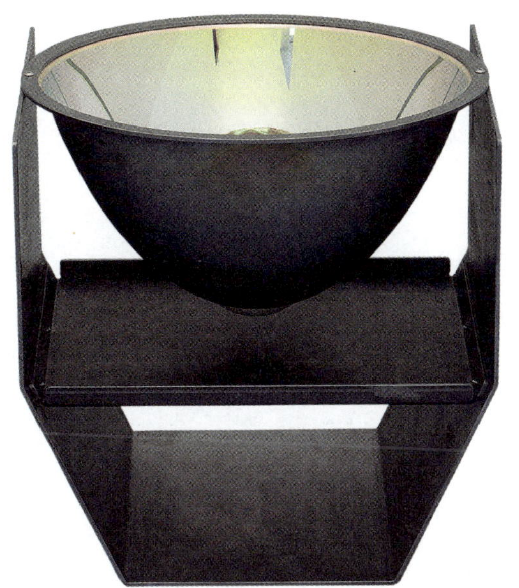

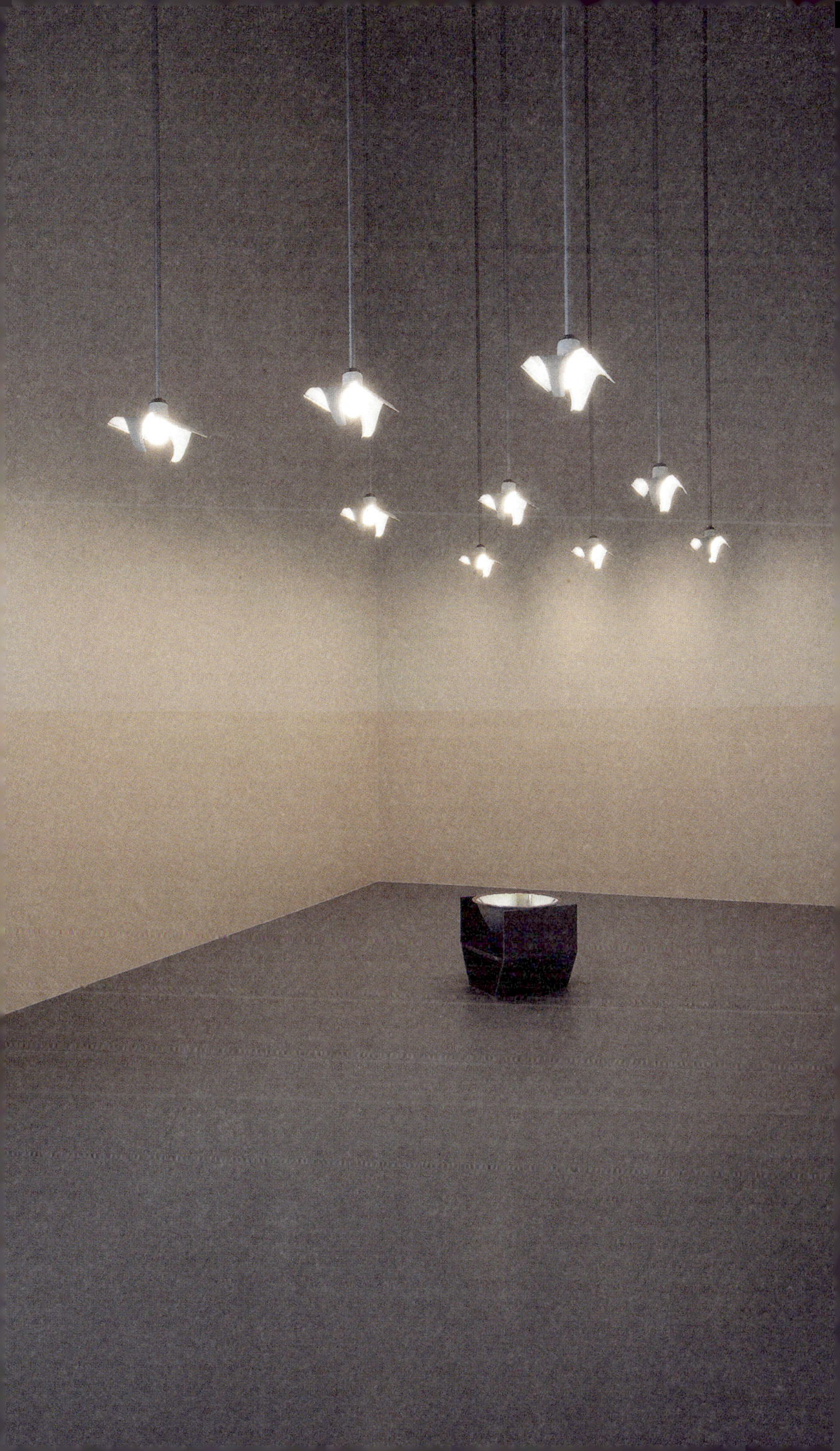

July 18–31

Artists Book (detail), 2010–23

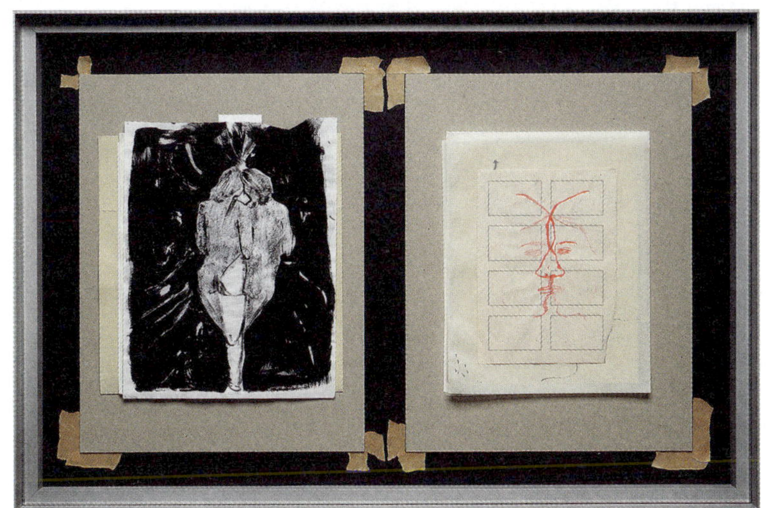

FAILURE, SHADOW, RECEPTACLE: NOTES ON *UMBRA (ETUI)*

Thomas Duncan

Perhaps we are gazing up at the moon through a deep-set window; thick clouds partially obstruct its light and produce jagged shadows on the jamb.

Or perhaps it is not the moon shining down but a lamp beaming up from the bottom of a littered pool, its light clawing its way through nebulous liquid.

Or perhaps the light comes at us horizontally, as if it were passing through a camera obscura, an enclosed room connected to the outside only by a pinhole that projects an upside-down image on its back wall. Photographs made with a camera obscura not only present down as up but also white as black; thus, our luminous orb may not be a moon or lamp but a black sphere hovering in a field of white light.

Or, or, or . . .

While none of these scenarios is true, the relations they conjure—between light and shadow, above and below, container and contained, interior and exterior—are essential to B. Ingrid Olson's set of *Umbra (Etui)* photographs.[1]

So, then, what are we looking at? Or, put another way, what is it that we *cannot* see? For three-quarters of what was undoubtedly intended to be a continuous image has been lost due to failures within the photographic process, which in this instance has produced an internal dye diffusion transfer print, more commonly referred to as a Polaroid. While emulsion smudges and ghostly spots are so prevalent in this form of instant photography that they are practically a given, the near-total failure that dominates *Umbra (Etui 03)* is rare. Such breakdowns betray what we could call a medium-specific beauty, for the cleavages and flourishes we witness in this photograph occur only with Polaroid film.

Failure does a lot of work in *Umbra (Etui 03)*. As if it were channeling Cubist collage, failure here suggests and undoes perspectival depth by juxtaposing and layering materials. Within the flattened space of the Polaroid, a ground layer comprises a partial image juxtaposed with a field of failed emulsion. On top of this ground is another layer consisting of two rust-colored bubbles, one of which doubly interrupts the failure and the image. Yet this failure-induced collage, impossible to have predicted, also has a strangely clairvoyant power. Its bubbles recall a microscopic view of human eggs, suggesting relations between photographic and biological reproduction that Olson has explored elsewhere. But I am getting ahead of myself.

So, again, what are we looking at? Or, put yet another way, what had Olson *intended* us to see? As a title, *Umbra (Etui 03)* offers us three clues. The first and second are the definitions of *umbra* as a shadow and *etui* as a container.[2] Thirdly, these photographs do not operate in isolation but in relation to one another. If we start with this last clue first, will the ten other photographs that come before and after *Umbra (Etui 03)* enable us to discern if she is the same as her sisters?

No.

Or yes.

When we look at *Umbra (Etui 02)*, we are privy to an entire image. The photograph offers neither a frontal nor upward-facing view but a downward-looking gaze at a sculptural construction. Its elements feel deeply familiar yet are challenging to identify correctly: On a piece of white paper rest three abutting components—a standing, visor-like piece of transparent plastic, a symmetrical calligram of black foam, and a clump of shredded memory foam or housing insulation or cotton stuffing or, or, or . . . Such is the sculptural foundation of each *Umbra (Etui)* photograph.

The artist shot her images both with and without the aid of a flash. With these twinned approaches, she exploits the phenomenological potential of the umbra and the penumbra. This shifts our perception of her assembled forms depending on the intensity of natural or artificial light. The photographs made without a flash accentuate the solid shadows from sunrays beaming through her studio's west-facing window. In *Umbra (Etui 11)*, for instance, sunlight passes through the transparent plastic that dominates the top of the frame and hits the flat and fluffed forms just below to create crisply defined shadows at the bottom. Conversely, *Umbra (Etui 09)*, made with a downward-facing flash whose vertical light intersects with the sun's horizontal rays, effects a penumbra, a partial shading caused by the flash's extreme mitigation of the solar-generated shadows.

These differentiated approaches to imaging sculptural constructions, however, do not speak only to the relation between light and shadow. Nor do they speak only to the sculptural relations between solids and voids. They speak also to the very nature of photography, as these exposures remind us that the shadow is a temporary form of inscription, an ephemeral occupation of space behind an opaque object with light shining on it. After all, photography is named after its essential element and the tracing of it: photo-graphy = light-writing. As Rosalind Krauss has famously argued, both shadows and photographs are traces or indexes of physical occurrence.[3] With Krauss's formulations in mind, Olson creates a photographic index of the indexical occurrence of the shadow—an index of an index, or, more abstractly, a photograph of a photograph. Thus, these varied manipulations of light operate as a performativity—a performed instantiation as opposed to mere description—of photography itself. But there is far more at stake here than self-reflexivity.

If *Umbra (Etui)* implores us to unpack the significance of *umbra* through serialized explorations of the index, how are we to think through the *etui* as a receptacle or container? For what would be the container here, and what would it contain? Certainly, the camera is a container, a lightless enclosure that opens itself up to the world to capture it only to return it transformed, whether enhanced or debased, in photographic form. In this sense, cameras and photographs are receptacles waiting to be filled. But does Olson use her photographs to exemplify the camera's capacity for containment? Or does she metaphorically tie the photograph-as-container to the very objects her camera records? Or both?

No.

Or yes.

What might the objects in these photographs say about containment, or tumescence, or embeddedness, or, or, or . . . ? We would do well to look again at the *Umbra (Etui)* photographs to assess the shape of the artist's black foam, which appears centrally in each frame. Its symmetrical protrusions and curvilinear base call to mind ovaries and a cervix, respectively. That this readymade foam object exists in photographic form complicates notions of biological and mechanical reproduction.

If this formulation seems somewhat strained, one need not look far in Olson's oeuvre to find the evocation of pregnancy—or the capacity to become pregnant—in repeated ovarian, cervical, and labial forms. While examples of such instances are too extensive to list here, it is worth mentioning the artist's *Door Picture, a view in perspective arranged close together*, 2021–22. This sculpture-photo hybrid comprises two photographic constructions housed both outside and within a white aluminum frame with vertical slits at the front and back that run from the base to the top.

The front aperture offers a perspectival view of *Door Picture, Penetration*, the photograph inside the larger structure. When seen head-on from the outside, the structure blocks the image save a view of a seated woman—the artist herself, surely—wearing pantyhose but no panties, with a phallic papier-mâché construction covering her genitals. As this construction is situated outside the nylon fabric she wears, it does not penetrate her. Instead, the photograph images the dynamic of possessing both a penis and a vagina, suggesting the actions of penetrating and being penetrated while documenting neither. Instead, the architectural exterior of *Door Picture, a view in perspective arranged close together* invites our gaze to pass through its slits—a suggestion of labial entry—toward a photograph that performs the denial of such entry. Just as the sculpture opens itself up, the photograph closes itself off. But we are ultimately implicated, for not only does our vision perform a penetrative act, *Door Picture, Penetration*, in turn, penetrates our vision. The entire work thus effects a performativity of both sexual penetration and the photographic aperture's processes of opening and closure. Yet, going even further, the two photographs within *Door Picture, a view in perspective arranged close together* depict the artist with a balloon tucked under her shirt, the classic play of pretend pregnancy, problematizing more deeply the connections between reproduction as biological (penetration with the potential for conception) and photographic (capture with the potential for duplication).

So why diverge into this analysis of *Door Picture*? When we return to the *Umbra (Etui)* works with *Door Picture, Penetration* in mind, we see another vaginal barrier underneath an ovario-cervical construction in the form of a clump of shredded memory foam or housing insulation or cotton stuffing or, or, or . . . The barriers in both *Door Picture* and *Umbra (Etui)* therefore present photographic and biological reproduction as forms of containment reliant on opening and closure, exposure and occlusion, access and refusal. Particularly valuable in this regard are the art historian and critic George Baker's recent assessments of Zoe Leonard's photographs of birds' nests holding unhatched eggs:

> And here the nests themselves—another "natural" avatar of the notion of a home, a place of birth or origin—were temporarily abandoned, and yet each was filled with waiting, potentially orphaned eggs: the receptacle of the nest filled with the container that is an egg, both of them filling the frame of the photograph, in a self-reflexive echo that also seems a kind of gentle manifesto, containers within containers within containers. Like the sun in photographs eventually to come, the eggs in these nests were never captured at the exact center of the image. Instead, the photographs remain subtle in their *endless differentiation*, as opposed to modeling a sense of repetition and replication—egg after egg, photograph after photograph, with natural reproduction compared to (and transforming) mechanical reproducibility.[4]

We may thus draw a parallel between Leonard's and Olson's association of biological containment with photographic capture. Even if we are to understand photographs, eggs, and wombs as containers, we still need to think through their attendant roles as instruments of reproduction. Much of the discourse that examines photography's indexical capacity focuses on the photographic negative, which produces a photographic positive through the inscription or indexing of light onto a photosensitive surface. More significantly, the indexical nature of the photographic negative offers a potentially infinite amount of duplication. In this way, photography is an instance of a simulacrum or a copy without an original.[5]

And yet Baker's formulations on Leonard's egg photographs—which the artist produced with black-and-white negatives—work *against* establishing a corollary between both forms of reproduction we have been discussing. If, as Baker posits, Leonard views the photograph as a receptacle and not as an a priori site of limitless duplication, this is also where Olson's and Leonard's concerns converge. If Leonard uses the negative to create what Baker refers to as "endless differentiation," Olson performs this with the negative-less, unique Polaroid. As such, her *Umbra (Etui)* photographs stress the "endless differentiation" of photographic originality. These Polaroids therefore operate within a kind of discursive paradox: Just as they call attention to the very fundamentals of photography, of its manipulation of light and its powers of inscription, their undeniable uniqueness resists the discursive fixation on photography's infinite reproducibility.

And here we arrive at what I meant when I asked if *Umbra (Etui 03)* were the same as her sisters and responded: "No. Or yes." For their differentiation instantiates what Jean-Luc Nancy described when he wrote that "the like is not the same."[6] Indeed, likeness distinguishes itself from sameness in such a way that it expresses affinity within difference rather than similarity without change (endless differentiation versus endless duplication). Likeness therefore presents us with "or" in the place of "and."

Should we thus view *Umbra (Etui)* as an exhortation of failure's potential?

Or can we view it as a treatise on the mutual indexicality of the shadow and the photograph?

Or should we consider it a twinned exploration of the body and the photograph as containers?

Or can we perhaps suggest that it operates as a prosthesis, an extension of the artist's very carnality?

Or, or, or . . . . . . ?

Or.

NOTES

1. While this essay focuses on a group of eleven photographs sharing the title *Umbra (Etui)*, it is important to note that in 2021 Olson made hundreds more bearing similar titles, such as *Umbra (Holder)*, *Umbra (Plastic Back)*, and *Umbra (Belly)*, each of which is reproduced in *B. Ingrid Olson: 323* (Berlin: Revolver Publishing, 2022). Unless otherwise noted, the nontitular information for all photographs mentioned in this text is as follows: B. Ingrid Olson, 2021, internal dye diffusion transfer print, binder's board, powder-coated aluminum frame, 16 × 12 ¼ × 1 in. (40.6 × 31.1 × 2.5 cm).

2. The *Oxford English Dictionary* (*OED*) gives one definition of *umbra* as "that portion in which the shadow is complete, as contrasted with the *penumbra*," which is the "partially shaded region around the shadow of an opaque body when the light source is larger than a point source and only part of its light is cut off (contrasted with the full shadow or *umbra*)." And the *OED* defines *etui* as a "small case, typically ornamental, for holding needles, cosmetic instruments, and other personal articles."

3. Rosalind Krauss, "Notes on the Index: Seventies Art in America," *October* 3 (Spring 1977): 68–81.

4. George Baker, *Lateness and Longing: On the Afterlife of Photography* (Chicago: University of Chicago Press, 2023), 53. Emphasis added.

5. See Krauss again, in her essay "A Note on Photography and the Simulacral," *October* 31 (Winter 1984): 49. See also Jean Baudrillard, *Simulacra and Simulation*, trans. Sheila Faria Glaser, The Body, in Theory: Histories of Cultural Materialism (Ann Arbor: University of Michigan Press, 1994).

6. Jean-Luc Nancy, *The Inoperative Community*, Theory and History of Literature, vol. 76 (1981; Minneapolis: University of Minnesota Press, 1991), 33. See also Jonathan Flatley, "Introduction: Like," in *Like Andy Warhol* (Chicago: University of Chicago Press, 2017), 1–52.

Iteration VI

August 1–28, 2023

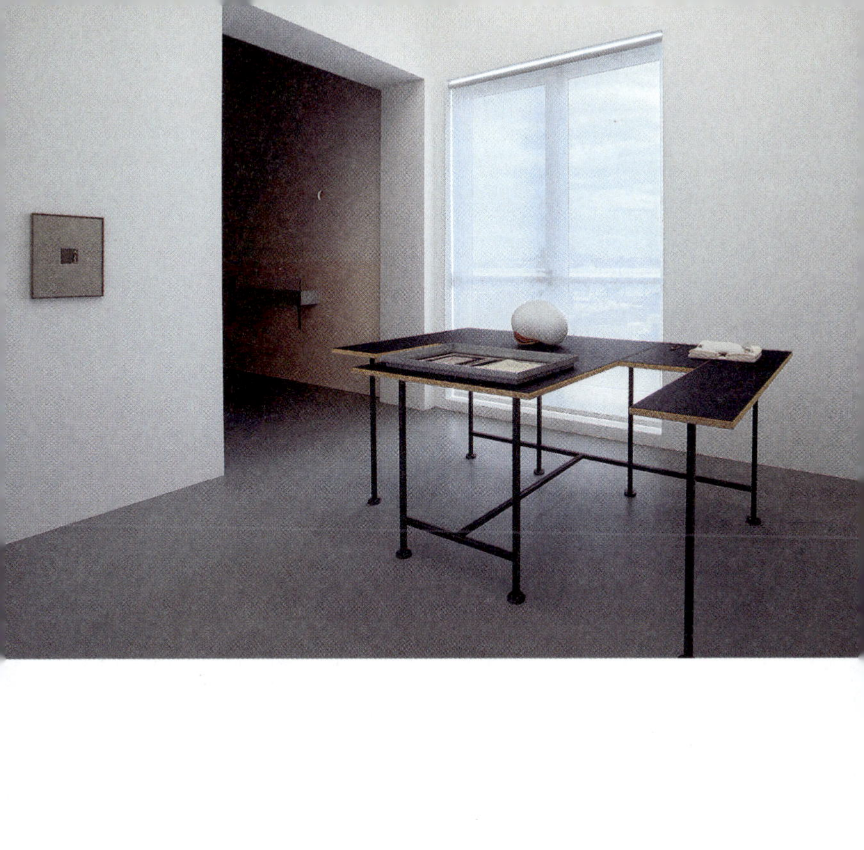

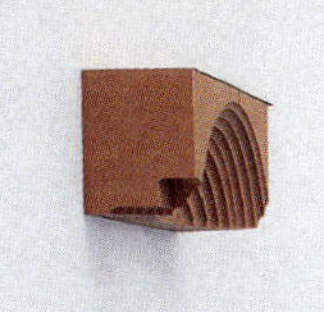

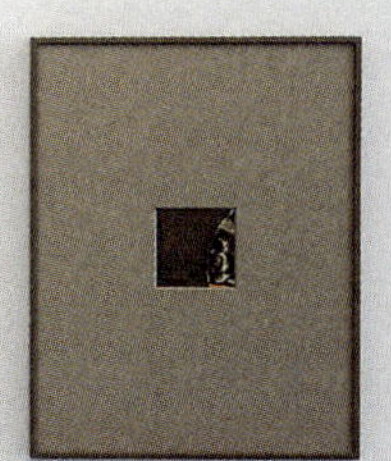

Forehead and Brain, 2018

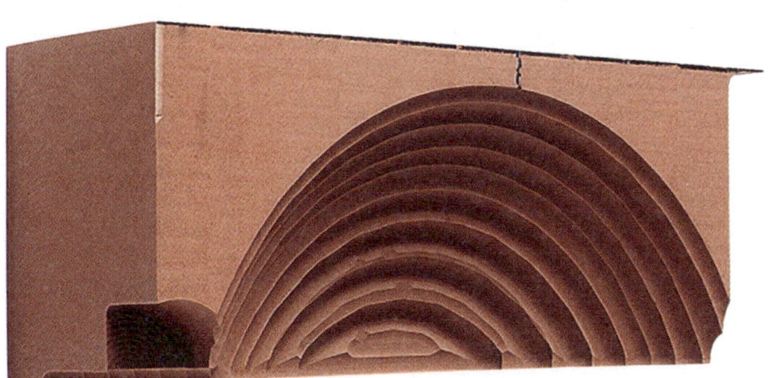

Umbra (Etui 03) (detail), 2021

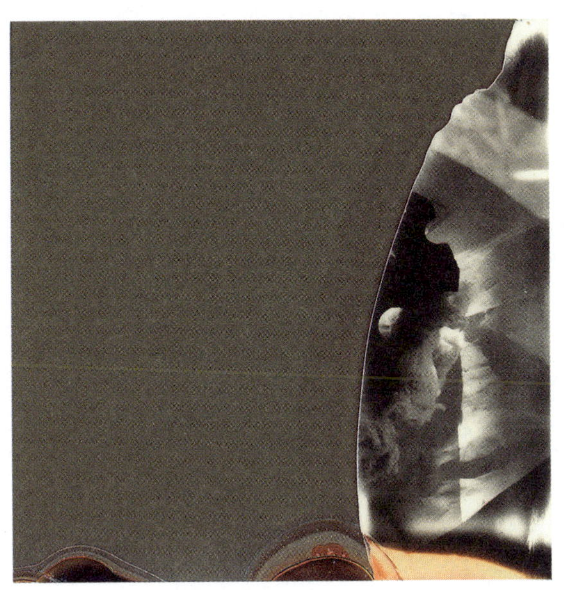

HEAD, HOUSE, LIGHT

Can a text be a house. Can a paragraph be a room. Can a sentence be a window. Wittgenstein's sister, Gretl, thought helping to design her large city house in Vienna would be a good activity for her brother, the philosopher. Wittgenstein was still recovering from the war, and, he thought, philosophy. He was working as an assistant gardener at a monastery outside of the city, and was mulling one of two possibilities for the future: either becoming a monk or committing suicide. He was in a form of exile, owing to what has been referred to as the Haidbauer incident, when working as an elementary schoolteacher at a village school in rural Austria, he hit an 11-year-old boy, one Josef Haidbauer, so hard on the head during class that the boy collapsed unconscious. There was a hearing, in which the judge requested a psychiatric examination—Wittgenstein fled, although he returned a decade later to apologize to the students, who were now older. Except for hitting the slower students, Wittgenstein was a wonderful teacher: he designed buildings and steamships with them, dissected animals, took long treks in the woods and identified plants, took the train to Vienna and discussed the various architecture of the buildings there. Even though he was a steel heir, he had given his fortune away, and slept in the kitchen, eating only oatmeal out of a pot he never cleaned. Of course, his family was concerned. There is a letter from his brother Paul, the one-armed pianist, to one of Wittgenstein's friends, worried that his brother was not eating correctly for his colitis. He was supposed to only assi[illegible] architect, who had studied under Adolf Loos, on the design of the ho[illegible] of those cold modernist constructions of three white cubes. He was p[illegible]rge of the interiors: windows, doors, doorknobs, and radiators. As befitting [illegible] fastidious philosopher who once studied aeronautical engineering, he became absorbed in the project and completely took over, even moving into the small architect's office to live there full-time. He had to design the door handles himself, which took him a year. The heights for the door handles were minutely designed according to door type. It took another year to design the radiators. Each of the large vertical windows was covered with a metal screen, moved by a pulley system Wittgenstein designed. He insisted that everything be designed according to exact proportions—including having the ceiling raised by 30 millimeters. He even wanted to make his own version of a head that he had disliked in one of the sculptures that were commissioned for the entrance way—his sister placed the plaster cast of the head he designed in the house. Of course, upon its completion, she didn't want to live there, and eventually the house was sold to the Bulgarian embassy. After finishing the house three years later, he returned to Cambridge and philosophy, wanting to work now on visual space. In his later *Philosophical Investigations*, he imagined thought as taking place in a room. "A person caught in a philosophical confusion is like a man in a room who wants to get out but doesn't know how." Wittgenstein himself liked to think in Spartan surroundings—sometimes a chair in a room was all that he needed.

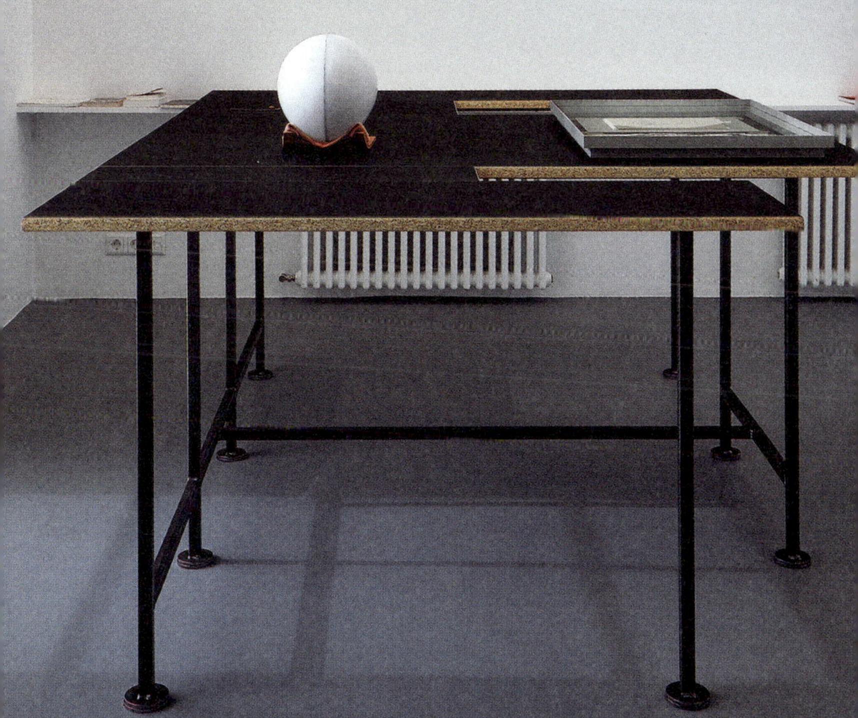

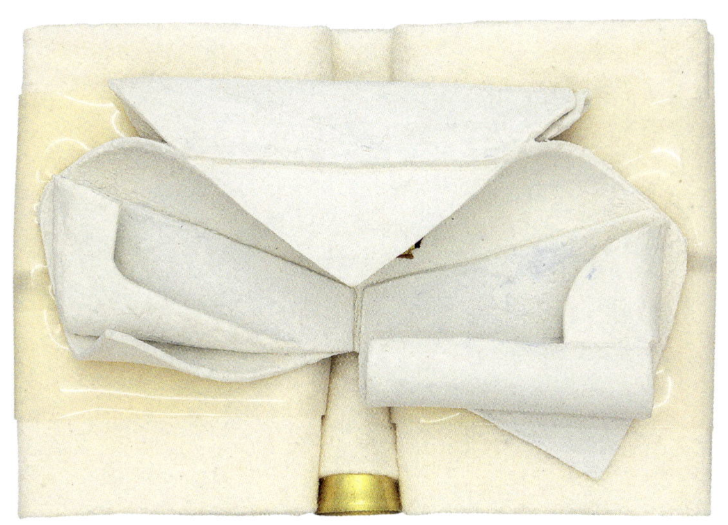

Artists Book (detail), 2010–23

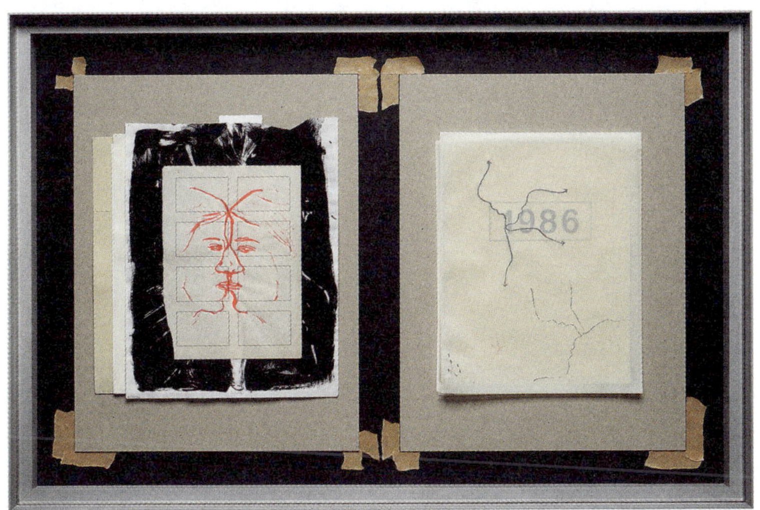
1986

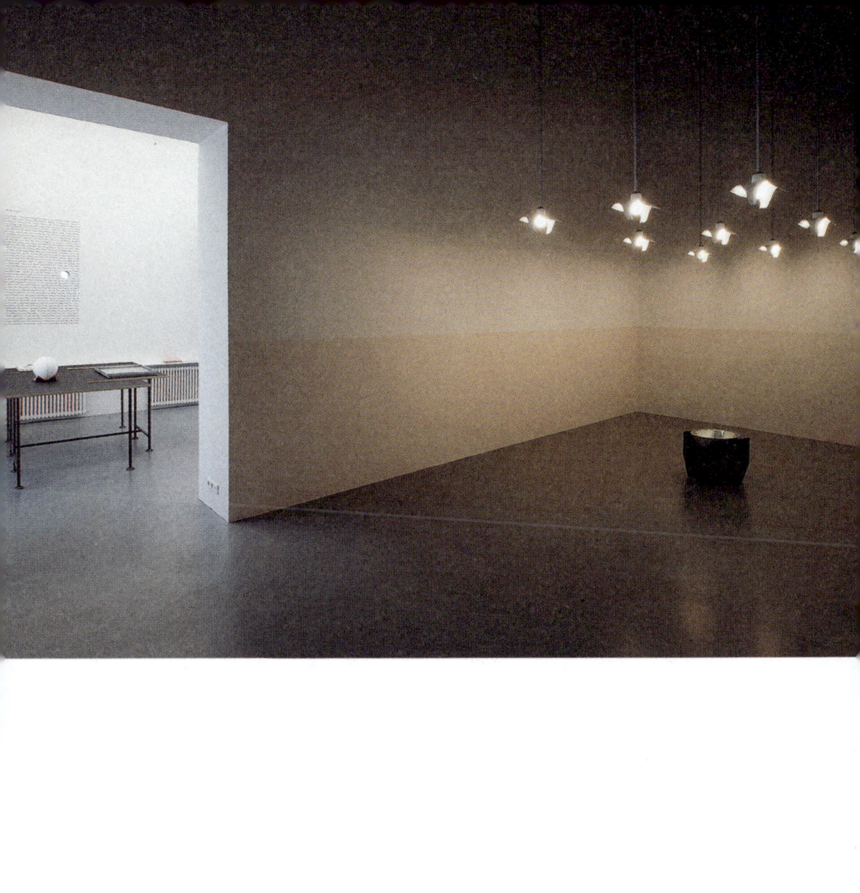

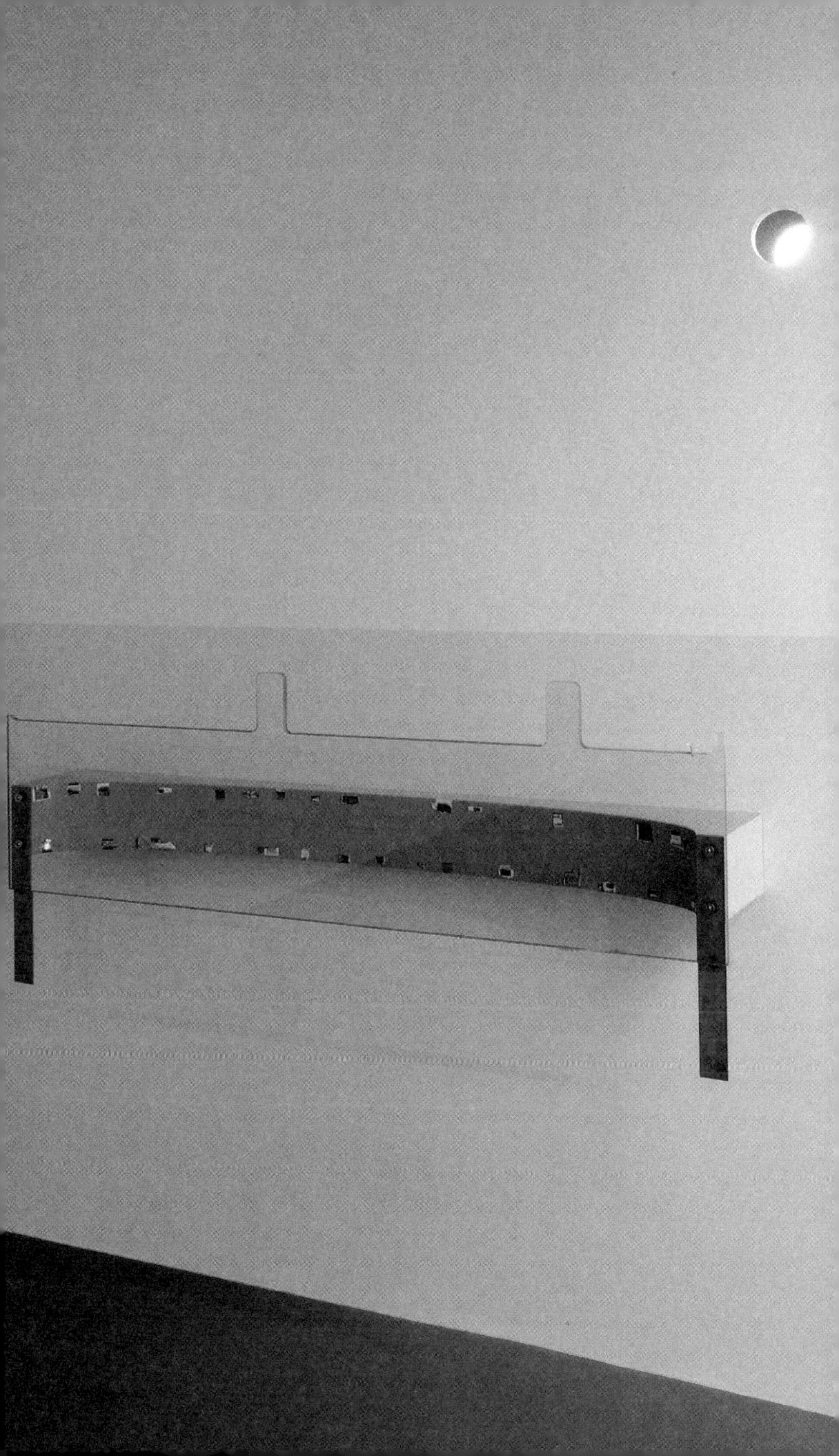

What I would be if I wasn't what I am, I, I, n.d.

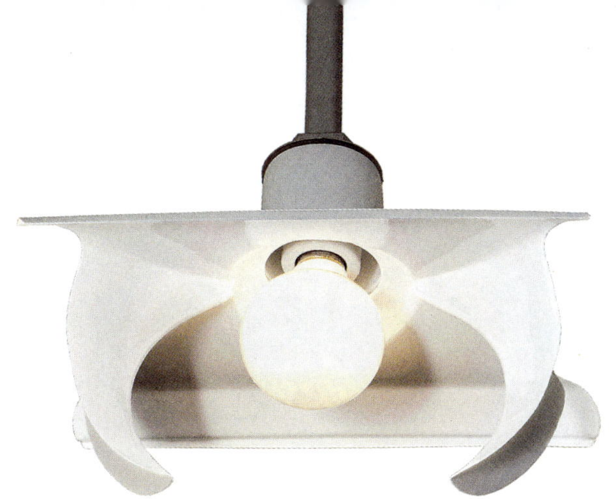

August 15–28

Artists Book (detail), 2010–23

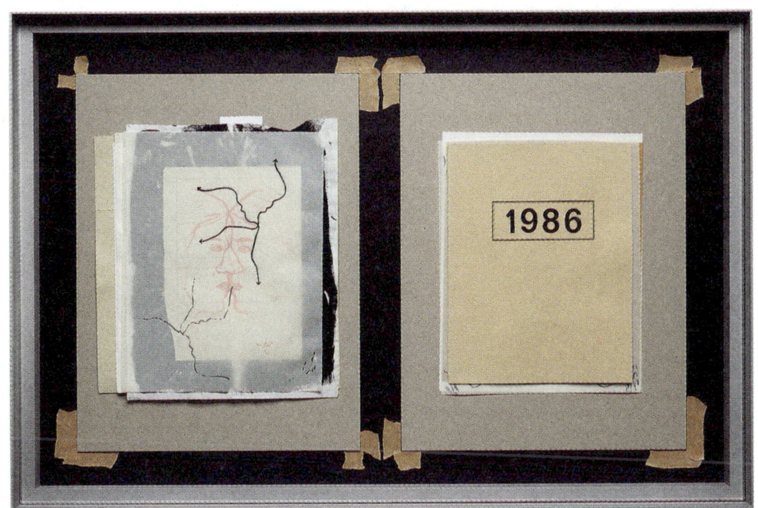
1986

CODA

Kate Zambreno

It is—I still maintain—strange to be asked to write about another in this way. Another woman artist, I mean. If that's what I am. Woman or artist. It's still in flux. Last week, when you were writing me, and I was trying to write you, I was seated on the train, bent over my phone, considering a cover of my book, in another language. Body twisted, hair flowing. That's not me, I said to the publisher. It doesn't have to be you, they said. It's in another language, another country. But what gender is she? Or am I? When I'm sitting here, at this table, thinking about this, I am neither and both at the same time. Perhaps I am you. Perhaps you wanted us to think together. That was intriguing, to imagine my body contorted in such a way, deep in thought, thinking of your work, thinking of my work through your work. There are so many doubles, mirrors, elective affinities. Both of us are folded over the table, in different rooms and times. I have found I can only write when upright at a solid table. Then still I can't really write. My neck is always stiff, sitting in this way. I take notes. I perform research. I suppose I could lie on the floor. In the other room, the living room. This table here and another table on the floor, in the other room. Books arranged on top of me. Time has seemingly elapsed, and it's been an entire year since you issued yet another intriguing invitation. How is that possible? That it's been one calendar year? What have I been doing? You were at a table, in a vastly different time zone, still deep in thought. It wasn't dark, although it was after midnight. It was full of light. I couldn't understand it. It felt alien, your life, how you traveled. I am at work on my laptop. Your website is so well done. It's such a bright and clean room. I forgot we emailed each other during this time. The you that wrote me one year ago, the you that wrote me those years ago, the me I was at those times, the I we are now. We write to each other of Bergson's duration. There are multiple points happening simultaneously. You most likely in your studio space, in another city, one I used to live in. I have started carrying around his *Matter and Memory* with me to different rooms. It sleeps on the table on the floor next to my bed. I write down notes that later I can't decipher—I make out "recollection as of a fold in a material." Perhaps, you write, I should reread it with you. I haven't read it in a decade. I am absorbed by the books that I read. They become part of me, as I know they do for you. That's my process. We agree that we read badly, we need to have the theory filtered second-hand. Who was the one who told the other to read Elizabeth Grosz's *Architecture from the Outside*? We can't remember. It was important to our thinking. One year ago, you wrote, I woke up at 3 a.m., jet-lagged. Something strikes me in my body. At 3 a.m. something often strikes me in my body as well, and I soak through the torso of my clothing. Then I sleep topless. The drawings of torsos also resemble your desk. It might be a good place, you write, to reignite our collaboration, if you feel stirrings.

(2022–23)

Even more time has passed. Years. It was seven years ago that you asked me to write these texts, that have hung on walls, in various rooms, including this brightly lit space I will never visit, although I received an invitation, for the opening, which I laughingly refused. Impossible to travel into your space, to leave my own. This is what I would like for you to do, you wrote me seven years ago, always so clear. Four pages, like a grid, like four panels of glass, almost like a window. These pages travel into other rooms, and live on those walls, that are then removed. A small bore of light enlarged over time, penetrating to become an actual window, living underneath. I wish for this to happen, for a small bore of light to penetrate my body, at the end, and to find out the book was within me all this time. I never even had to write it. That sounds like science fiction. Someone else, a frequent collaborator, emails me—the speculative novel is spatial. There is a map. It is how we think together, how we live and blur into each other, side by side. I have questions. I am trying to understand. Something I wrote in one room is now in another room, and then in another room. I am now in another room, considering what I wrote in that room. Is that correct? Something like that. I look into the other room, the one where apparently there is living. There are no boundaries between live/work space, not for me. Perhaps for you. Yes, definitely for you. I see the couch, but it is not exactly the same couch in which I wrote those texts, nor am I the person that I once was, but it is a similar enough couch, cheaper, came in a box. I know on the wall will be your work that you gave me. Whenever I sit on the couch I regard this image. It is the only piece of art, from someone outside, that we own. It has lived in different rooms. For a while it wasn't here. Then we had to go live somewhere else. The mirrors across the lap. The reiteration of the crotch-like ceramic sculpture. Mirroring. One image is embedded in another. The she is headless, yet posing with a camera above the frame, wearing a leotard and tights, recording the body as it moves. There are multiples of her. Crotches, splayed legs, torsos, feet, knees, elbows. The body is subject matter but the I is not a subject. Yet there is a mystery. I don't sit in this room, on this couch, anymore. Not like before. This room is actually another room, but it's the same room. A similar room. Everything is laid out basically the same, the same spatial orientation. The walls are white and bright, but they will also become shabby over time. The couch as collapsible body. Yet I feel confused, thinking about this room and that room, as I look into the other room, like into the past. My space enters your space. Your space enters mine. There is a doubling feeling. Who was I then? I'm struggling to understand. I really should lie down soon. I'm exhausted, sitting up in this way. My shoulders. Back. Feet arched. But once I do, this session is over.

(2017, 2023)

This is my language, I think, then feel spooked. Did I write this? I recognize it as one of your titles. Do you recognize your titles in the texts that I've written for you? Of course you do. It's fairly obvious. I have no idea where I wrote this—"I was then a we." I wasn't speaking about us, together, but could be now. A retrospective feeling fills me, reading these words I apparently once wrote. For instance, I have no recollection that I was reading *The Passion of GH* at the time, in that other room or series of rooms. Seven years later, I am still attempting to read it. No, literally, it was open on my table as I reread my words. Then I felt doubled again. The speaker feels disorganized. She has lost her form for hours and hours. Let's say: years. Can one be like a child again and stay lost? The room becomes an unstable place. Who else can enter and become other than one's self? I have a handout I've been carrying with me from room to room: "The Seven-Year-Old Transformation." It begins a new cycle every seven years. The first seven years a child "takes hold" of their physical body. This gesture can include the changing of teeth. New teeth indicate that the transformation is almost complete. There is a new body. New life force that allows for memory, abstractions. After all, cells are replaced after seven years. Now the child's own body is a "protective garment." OK. This significant change is shown through skipping, jumping, other proprioceptive input. Are we hanging on to our children and not letting them grow, freely, like a butterfly? But it's not my body either, anymore. This is a different body. There is no getting my body back. After seven years I'm not the same body at all. The body is in flux. There is rapid turnover. Amazing to realize that when I first was tasked with thinking about your work I had a newborn, who was still just newly outside of my body, our body, the small iteration clung to my large frame, us both lying on the couch, propped with pillows, and now I have a seven-year-old. You must know when to step forward and when to step back, the handout tells me. All this time has passed since I sat at a desk. It's been seven years since this has been my practice. Lying prone. On couches, beds. Usually with growing babies on top of me. All the iterations of babies on top of me. Bellies then babies. There is a fairly large child sleeping on top of me now. We are in the last months of this. And then what? I am just an I? No, no, I am still a we, various in my multiplicity.

(2017, 2023)

Are you writing a persona? a student asks. Is each book a different self or subject? I don't know. I don't think so. It is always not me. I cease to be. I become someone else. As you might imagine, this doesn't fit neatly into categories of nonfiction and fiction. I feel closer to your work now than I did before. Sometimes I feel closer and sometimes I feel farther away. To my own work as well. These writings on the wall feel close today. It seems to me you are allowed such freedom, the student then said, possibly irritated. Well. Yes. But I am still here, circling. What is your subject position? It changes. It moves around. I read online summaries of an ancient text on hysteria. Compressions. The womb, it wanders. It is searching for fluid. It wanders around the body like an animal. The worry, that it caused suffocation of the mother. This womblike thing floats, switches places. The baby wanders out of my womb and onto my body, then the floor, now standing on top of tables. Perhaps what I'm moving around to try to find is a window. But then I'd have to clean it. Vinegar mixed with dish soap. The last time when the placenta came out, the midwife asked if we wanted to see it. It was like its own apartment or house, stretched out. A house within my body, another being dwelling within me. The Lispector heroine is always a housewife, sometimes a rich one. The claustrophobia of her interiority, as well as her actual domestic space. She is disgusted by the thought of how filthy her maid's room will be once she enters it. I can't write you back yet, you write to me, of my endless list of questions. Laundry day. As it goes, for me, every day is that as well. Feels like something, to write that to each other. Eva Hesse complained in her diary of having to do laundry. She has to do laundry, he doesn't. There is no life/work division. It's all within the home. Recollection as if of a fold in a material. The bra I'm still wearing hanging around the house, slumped over my laptop, is an inside bra. It's a soft bra I purchased during that first inside period, off the internet. It is not new anymore, as advertised. It is old and stretched out. I am wearing my maternity pajama pants from that first pregnancy. That is what I've retained, worn-out clothes I once bought on the internet. It took six months, even then, my archives tell me. Six months of thinking of your work to be able to write these four pages, these four rooms that opened out into other rooms. Another line stops me, I think some part of me once wrote it, some other self. But I could be mistaken, it could be another text that I've internalized—"Can it be that I am the subject?"

(2017, 2023)

Iteration VII

August 29–September 20, 2023

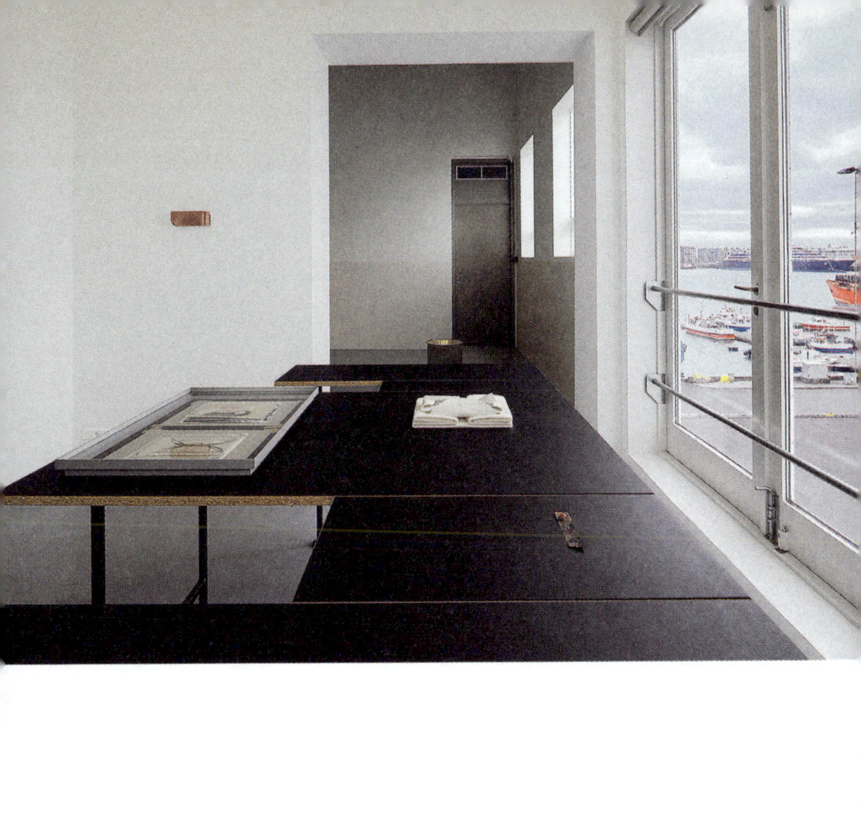

Total Work (Cast of Mind), 2023

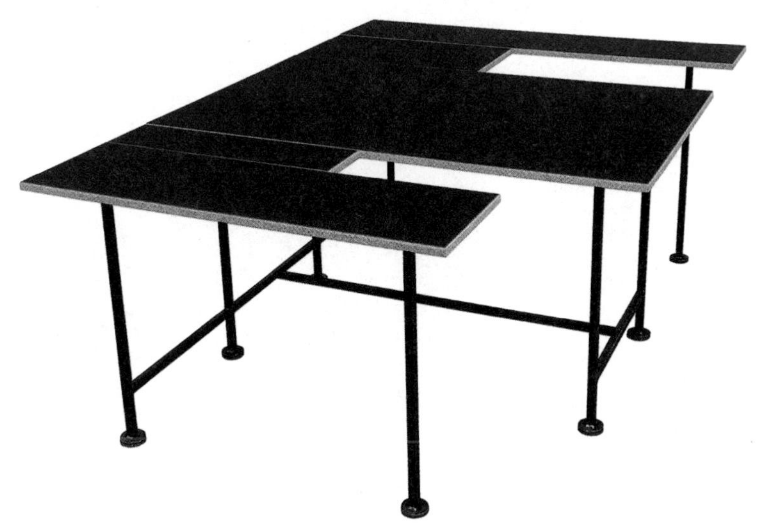

Artists Book (detail), 2010–23

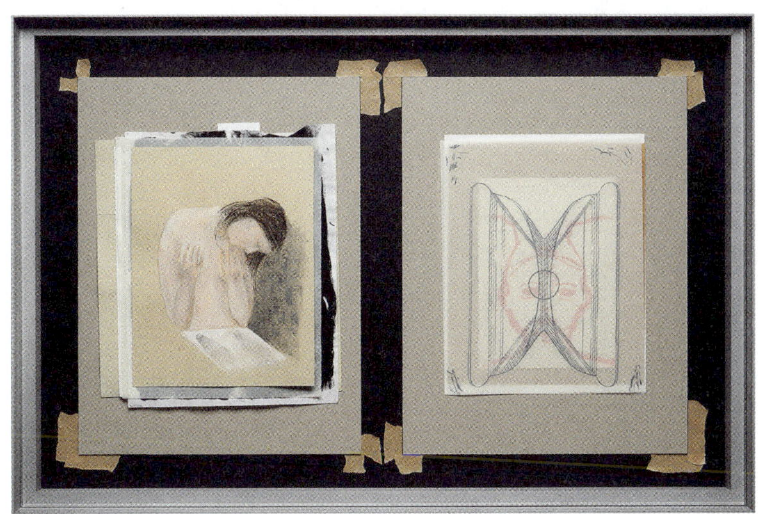

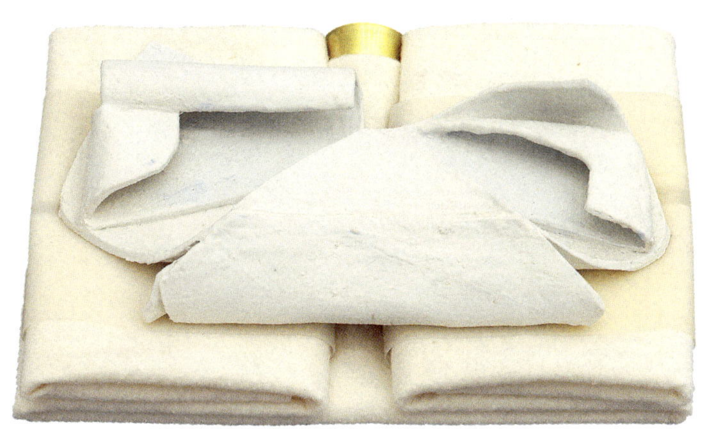

Forehead and Brain, 2018

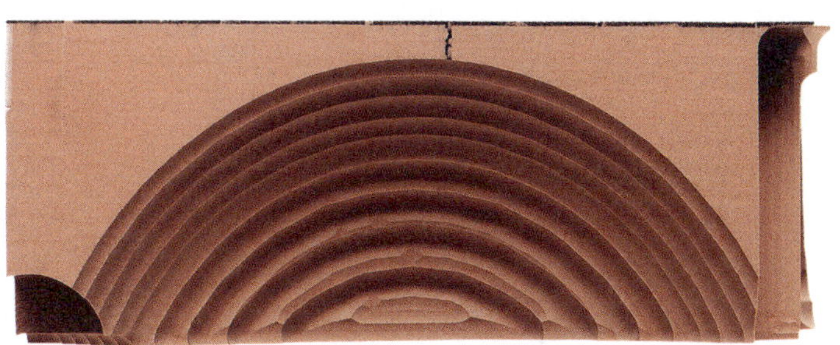

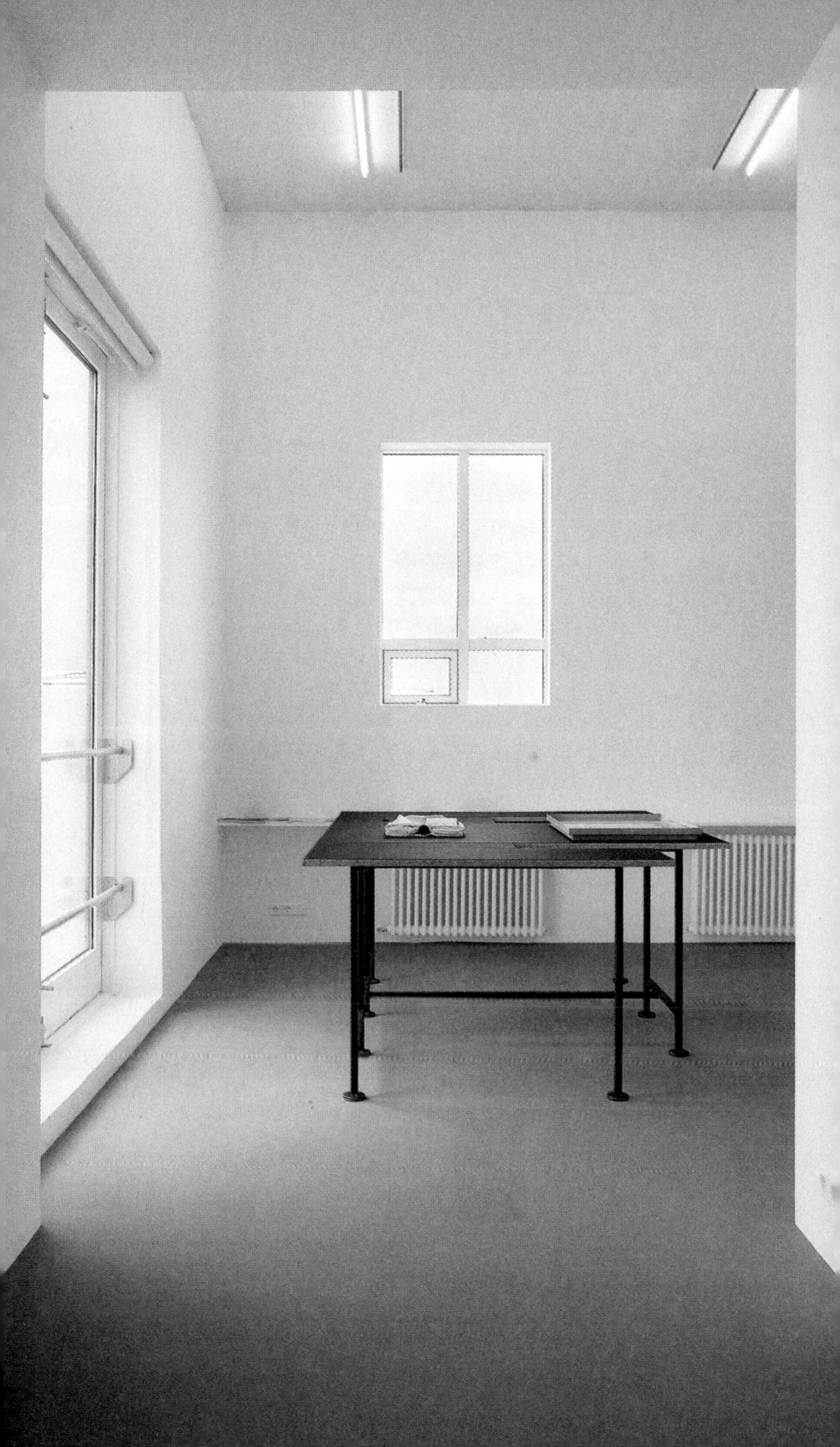

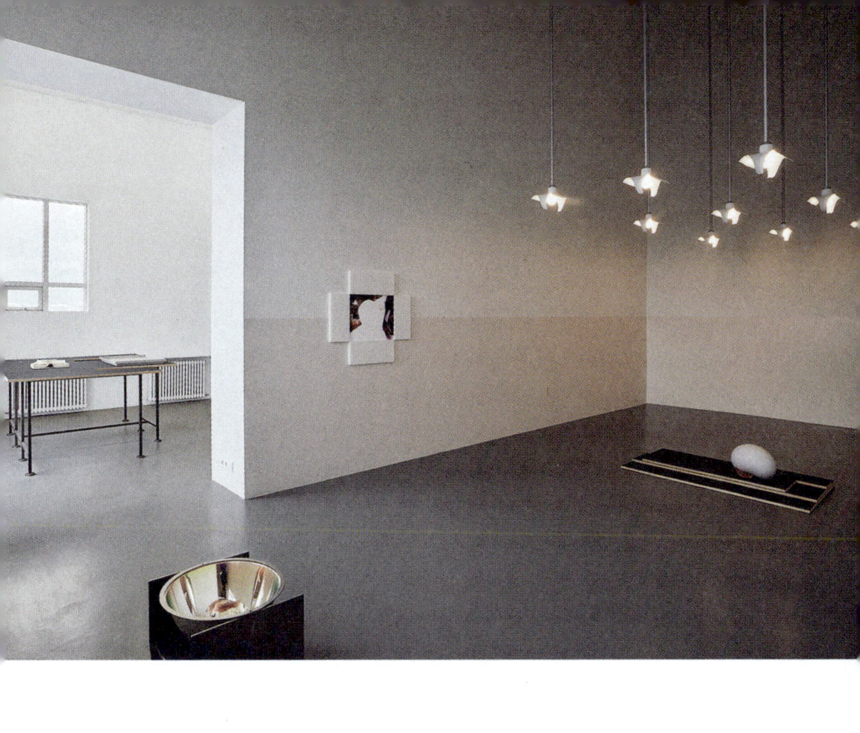

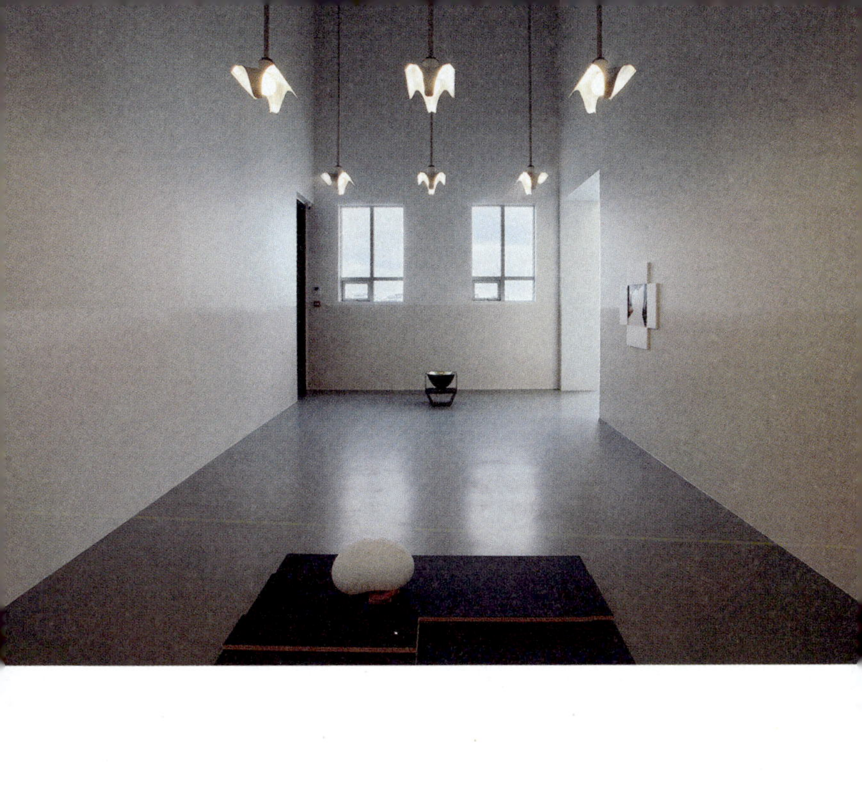

Reflective Comedy, standing shoulder wall, 2023

Total Work (Rest), 2023

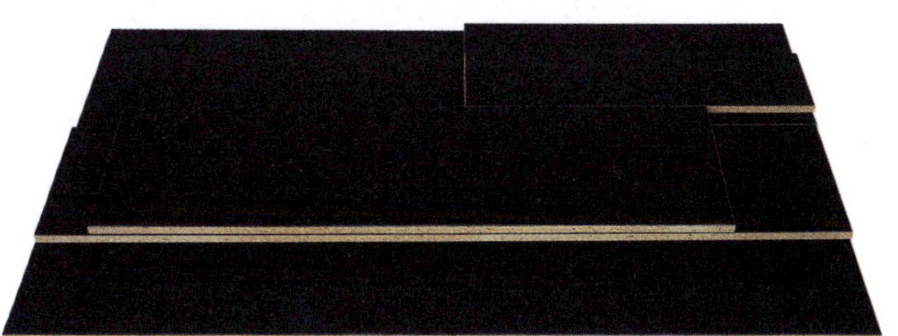

Standing Picture (present/present), 2021

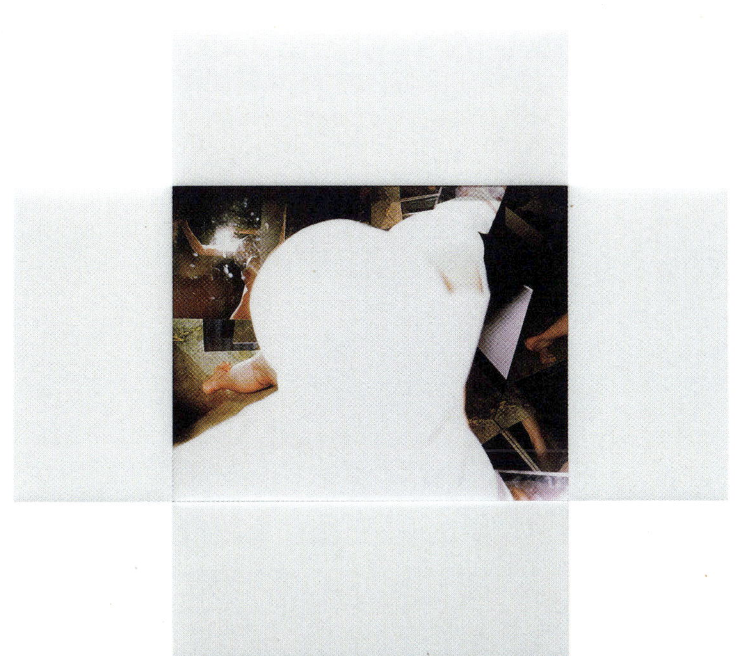

Plen, cycle, 2022–23

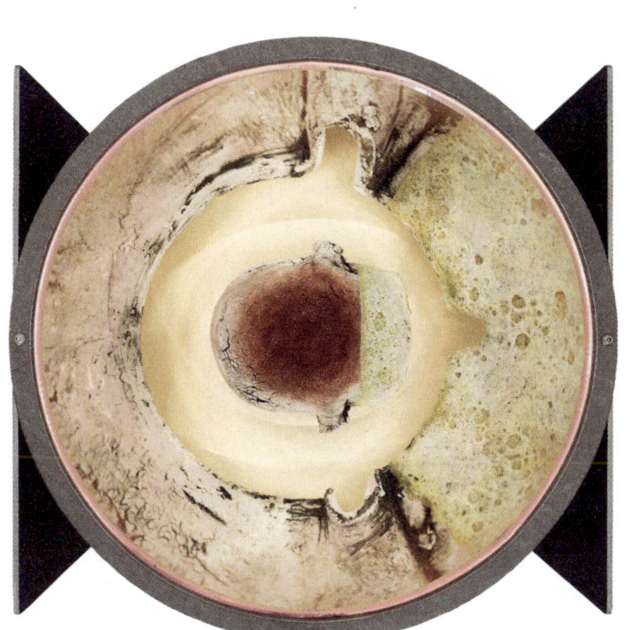

EXCERPTS FROM *TEXTURE NOTES*

Sawako Nakayasu

10.9.2003

Start from the outside of a peephole, and how much time it takes. The long way includes a beer mug, half a centimeter of green tea inside, a pair of glasses, needs replacement, salad bowl, bathroom window, does the mirror count, a jar used in performance, it used to contain ants, poor things, the lens in a borrowed video projector, internal glass door, second internal glass door, some component of a pen, or was that plastic, some component of a picture frame, yes it is glass, something under my skirt, no that is not, mason jar with sauce, mason jar with foreign Asian money worth very little, some component of the phone, somewhat likely, some component of the television, the bedside table swivels into three, the mirror from the neighbor, a sentimental picture frame, but the other one is acrylic, the last picture frame, it is small but empty, a place saved for my grandfather, and then now, here, the last sliding glass door or two, all of it melting and meltable, all of such heat and where it could accumulate, what it takes to melt, what the idea of "all" really amounts to, what "melt" involves, as opposed to my heart melting is not a good thing, hey you, making your way out the opposite end of some small amplified hole of glass.

11.12.2003

for Ray Nakazawa

After stepping out of the room chock-full of sneakers, and the need for fresh air.

Something compels us towards the room of eyeballs. It is either that time of year again, or somehow they have managed to become "all the rage," "the hottest thing," "cutting edge," "in."

And in we are, a room, a wondrously giant room, filled to the rim with a lifetime supply of eyeballs, equally giant as befitting the room. "Eyeballs as big as your head," I'd heard mention of in a guidebook for some faraway country. It made me feel like a hick for all those burritos "the size of my head" I used to eat, back in San Diego.

Whose eyes? What kind? Tuna, we naturally decide, as we swim merrily along through the muddle of vision, every which way a stare, a gaze, no body part immune from regard, no part free from that external, organic, dead and steady pulse.

11.15.2003

for Shoshana Michael

A pickup truck, or the process of letting it go.

The trick is, she reminds me, to never let it get too hermetic, to leave the window cracked, that dent unfixed, and even better, if you can stomach it, to get yourself a pickup truck and get used to driving it, find a comfort at every speed, and then, after having mastered all that driving—which includes stopping, parking, head-on, tail-first, three-point turns, twenty-seven-point turns, immediate and perfect and elliptical circles and donuts and pinwheels, oh my, backing out of a narrow and longer-than-usual driveway, stopping and having an extended conversation with someone out the window while keeping your foot on the brake the whole time—piling it in, piling it on, everything at any given point, in the cab, in that space behind the seat of a short-legged driver, in the inches of air above your head, piling it in with every which kind of breath and intention, further, piling in, on, back, out, while only slowing down, yielding to the additional weight of more and more, and all of it filling the infinite back of the pickup, taking it all on as if it were nothing, keeping the foot steady, tender, still, on the gas, wait until the piling-on of it never gets to its final conclusion nor fulfillment, no ceiling no end not even edges, no, the round and infinite surface of the outside of the back of the pickup a dark gray shiny pickup, everything all the intangibles and all the cities all piled up still and further in the growing small space back of the truck, tailgate busting up and still you drive on the freeway and observe through the rearview mirror—

What it is that stays, or rather sticks, and the rest of those things which fly away, tiny or medium-sized fragments of matter yes they do matter or do they quite a bit which is why you keep driving, with your eyes both on the front and on the mirror as you go and go and go on, this way that way any any any this moment rather than the last.

10.29.2003

Traffic of the internal plumbing.

Scales of imbalance. Left at the neck. Please clear.

Or if the jam could err to the sweet.

Iteration VIII

September 21–October 30, 2023

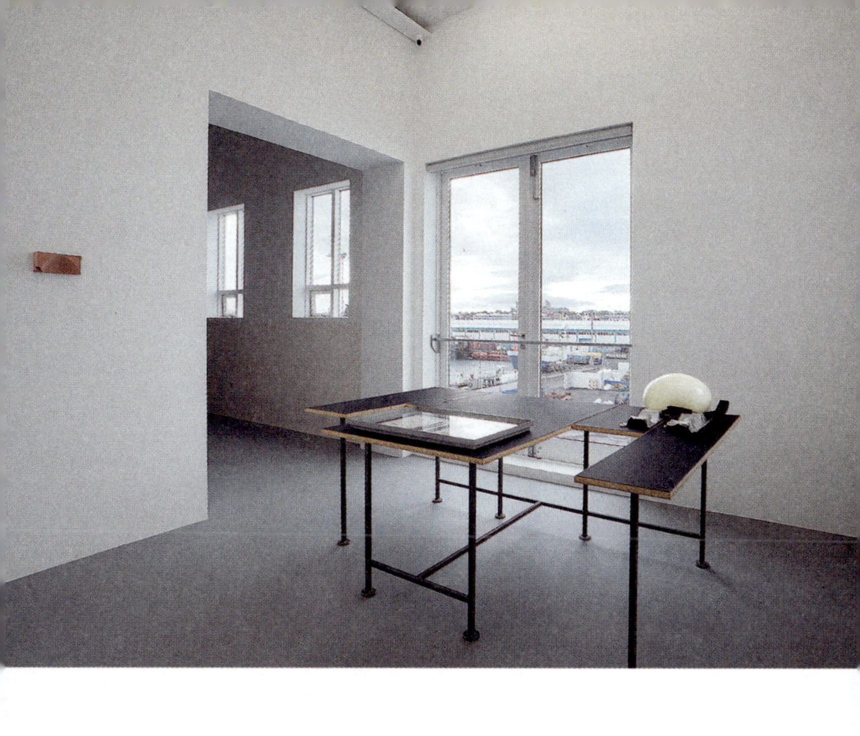

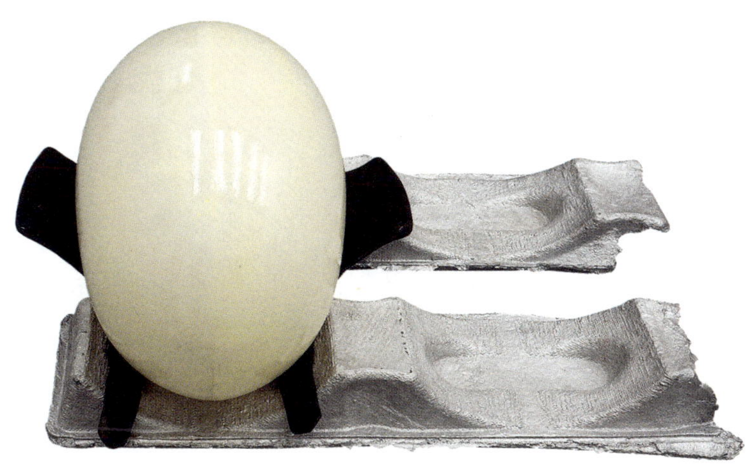

Artists Book (detail), 2010–23

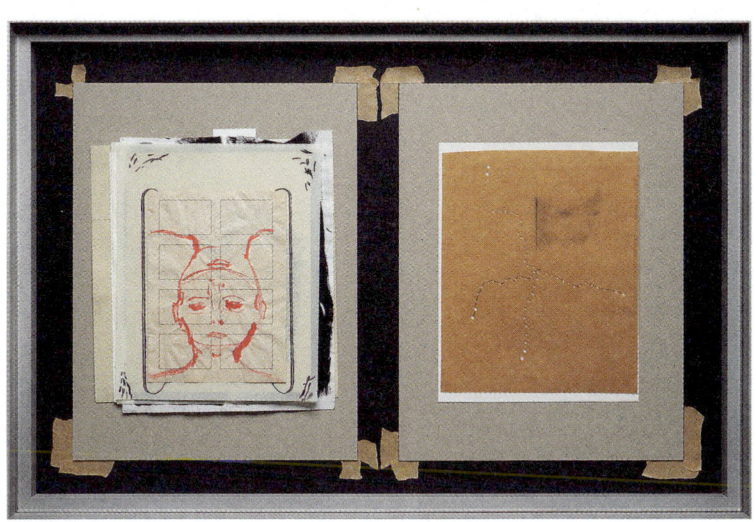

Clock / Painting, 2023

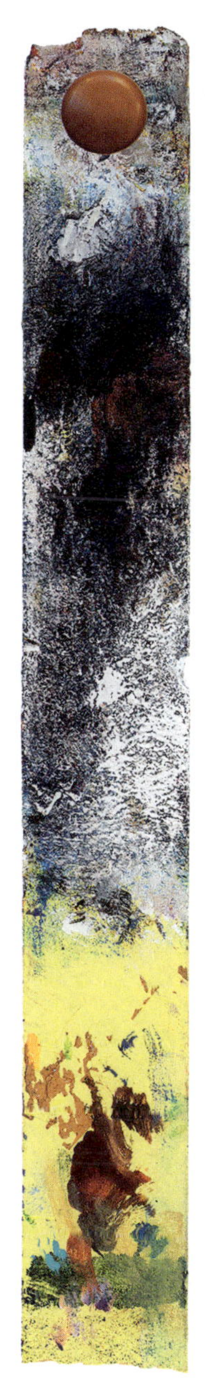

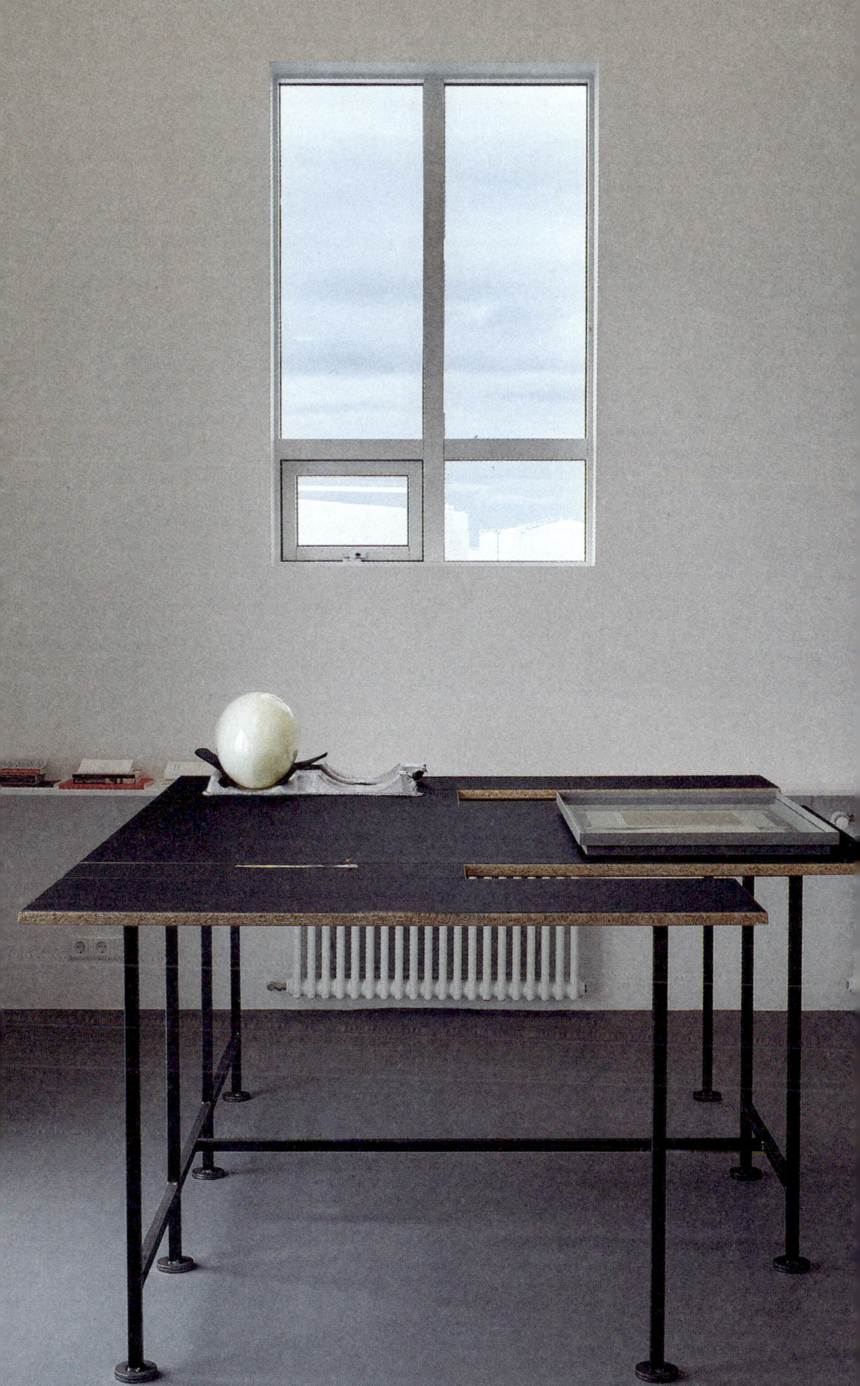

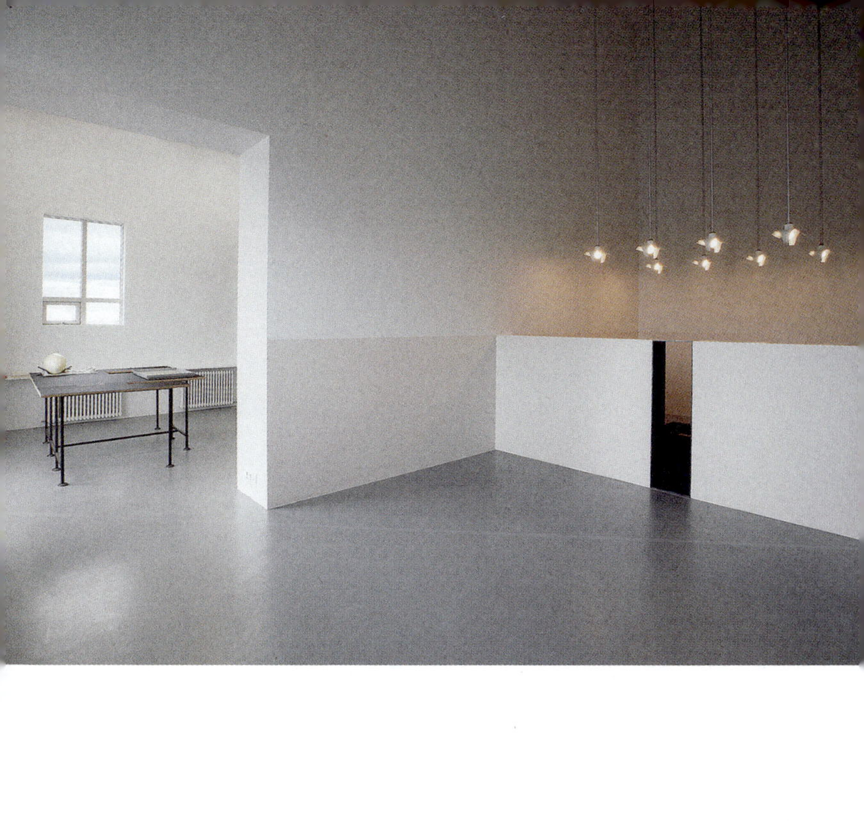

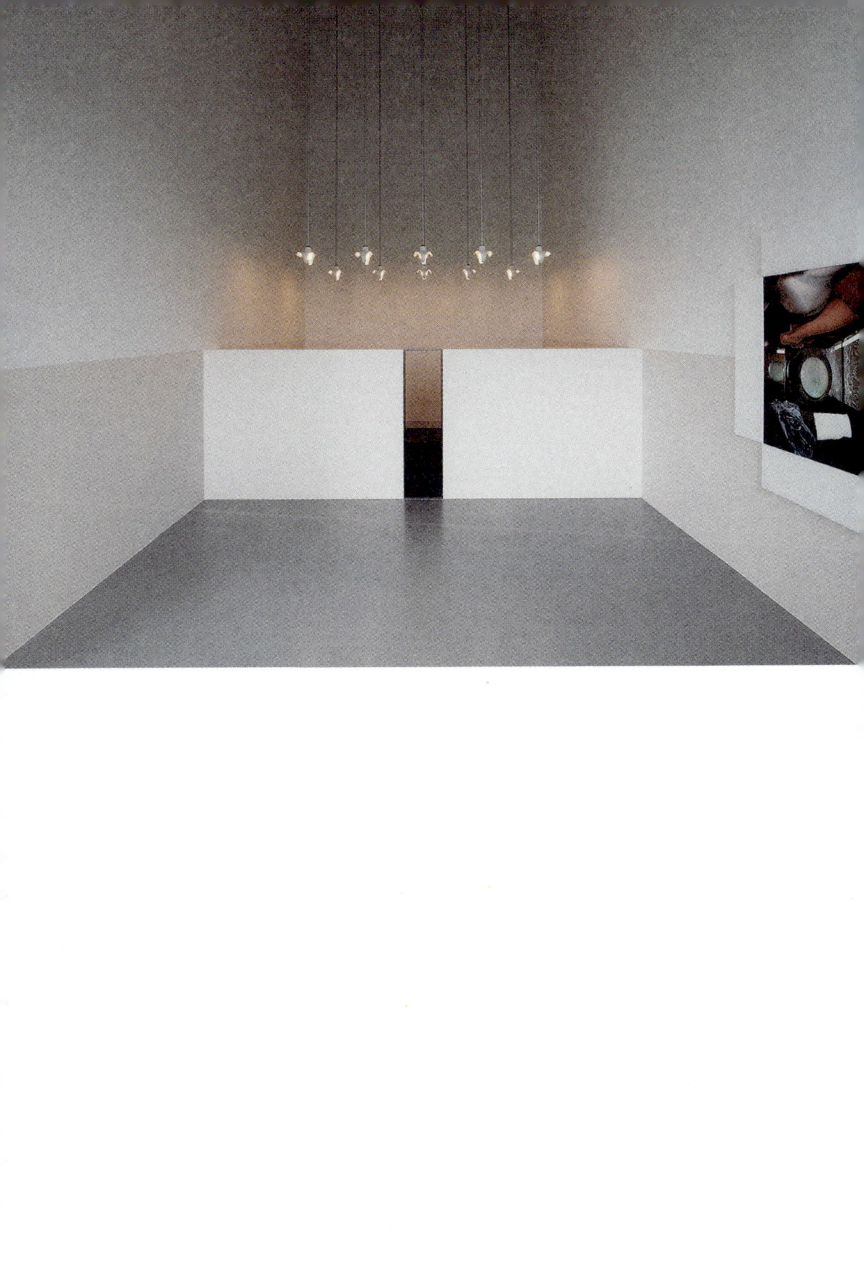

Sluice (A weird rewriting of negative capability?), 2023

Round Room (present/present), 2022

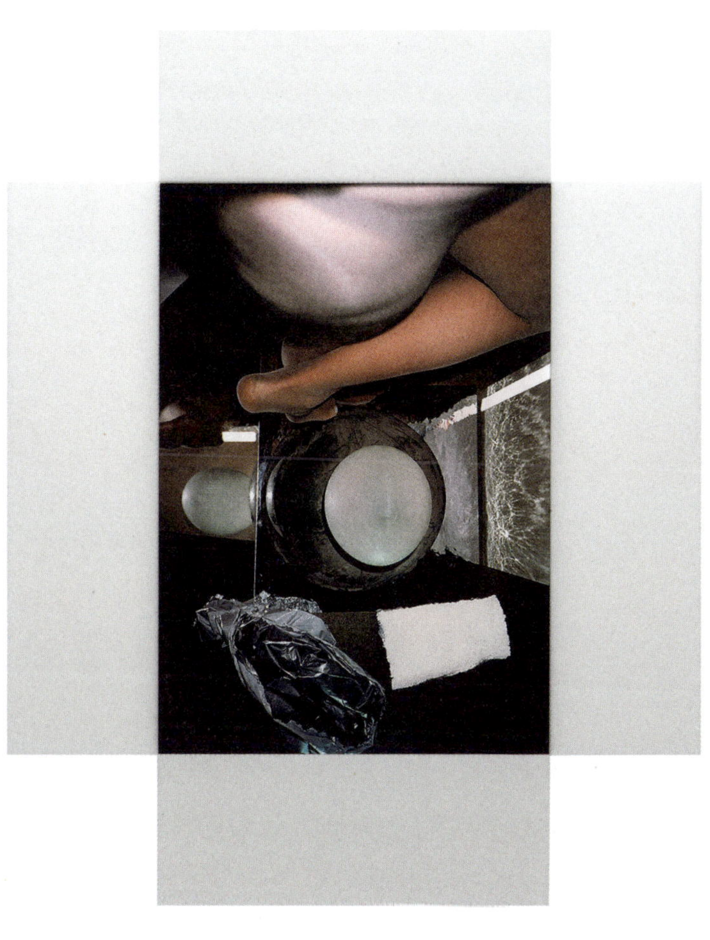

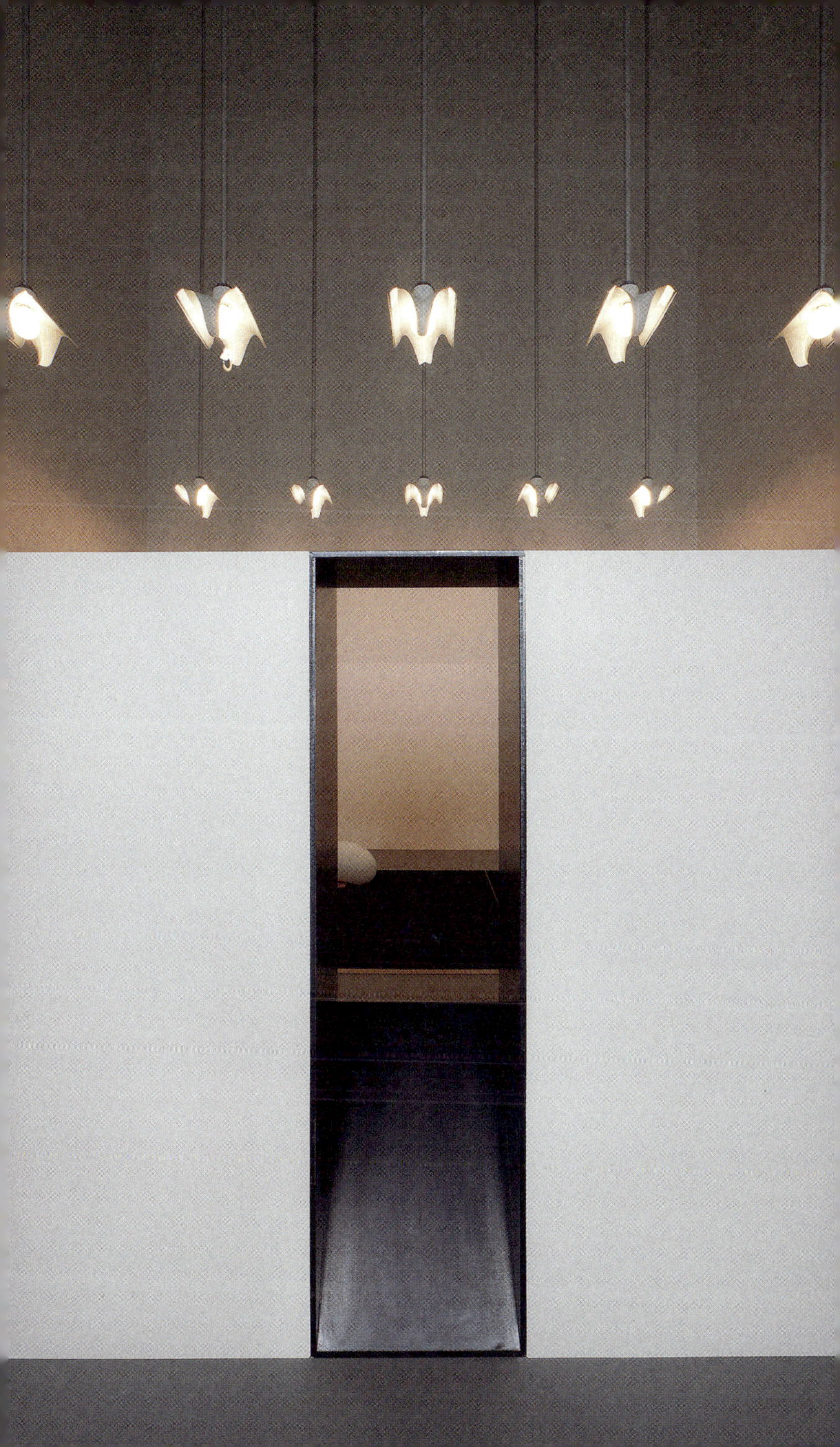

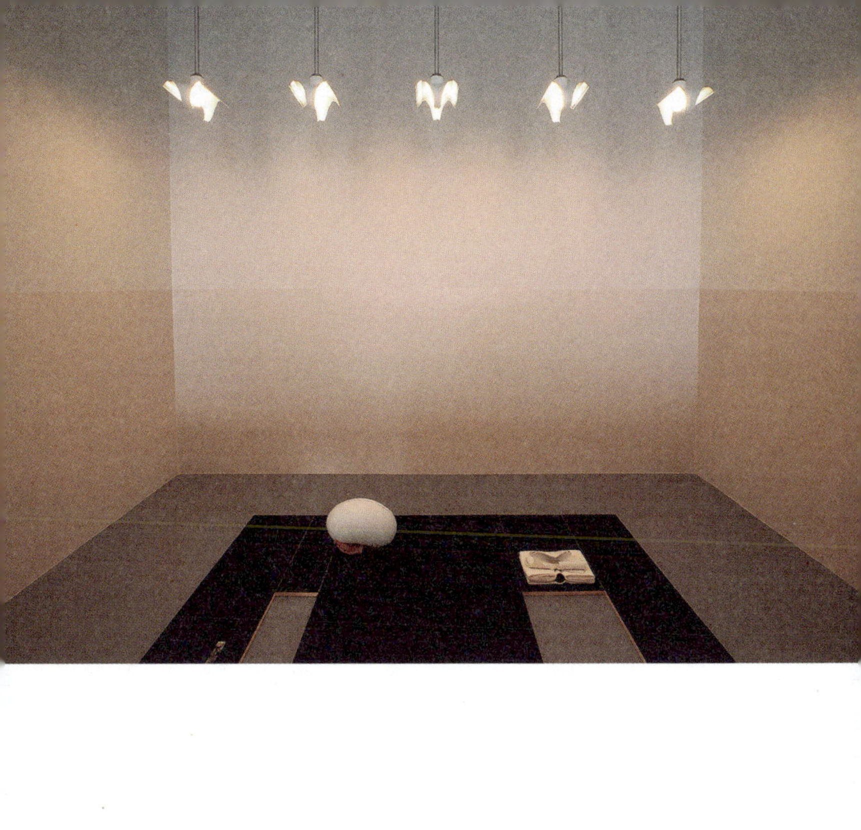

A HOLDING IN PLACE

Mariana Fernández

Does the body play a constitutive role in cognitive processing? How do properties of the body constrain our model of the world?
—Thomas Metzinger

In the dream state, the mind is asleep and the physical body is fully paralyzed—as Metzinger describes it, dreamers are disembodied agents.[1] Sleep paralysis, however, occurs in a dissociative transitional state between sleep and wakefulness when the brain fails to integrate the body's sensory feedback during the Rapid Eye Movement (REM) stage. The sleep paralyzed experience a hypersensorial form of bodily consciousness despite, or even because of, the impairment of movement. The brain is active, but the body is immobile, and sensory input begins to misfire: The body cannot make sense of itself in relation to its surroundings, leading to a phenomenological rift between mind and embodied self, a breakdown in self-consciousness.

Walter Benjamin gives another name to the feeling with his dialectical image: a moment of frozen contradiction—static, like a dream image, yet pulsing with latent motion.[2] B. Ingrid Olson's work unfolds at this space of cognitive estrangement. Her images disrupt spatial coherence, unmooring familiar settings and dissolving the body's stable position within space.

"The dreamer does not know that he is dreaming."[3]

The architecture of *Cast of Mind* is located in the body, somewhere in the gut, but begins in the mouth. The small room one encounters upon entering the gallery is almost completely filled by *Total Work (Cast of Mind)*, 2023—a semifunctional worktable, sculpture, and stage for a shifting configuration of artworks and books that viewers must circumvent within a narrow perimeter. On the walls, photographic collages of Olson's body warped by mirrors, shards, and writhing contortions contribute to a sterile sensation of confinement. Here begins a durational exercise in perception and embodiment. Like an involuntary imitation of dream paralysis, *Cast of Mind* engages the built environment in an interplay of materiality and flatness; time and space are flexible, expanding and contracting through configurational convolutions.

From March to April, the surface of *Total Work (Cast of Mind)* held a copy of Madeline Gins and Shusaku Arakawa's *Architectural Body*, a poetic manifesto putting forth the idea of a phantom-like species or matrix or shell—the "architectural body"—collapsing the human body and its direct environment. Rather than conceiving of the built environment as a passive space to simply inhabit, the pair's architectural projects were designed to alter human perception and consciousness, even mortality. Of their Bioscleave House in East Hampton, New York, with its uneven floors and sloped walls, the artists claimed that its "fundamental subject is staying alive/coming alive/staying alive to. Thanks to the architectural procedures this house has in play, whoever moves about within it wishing to live forever may do so."[4]

In Olson's work, architectural interventions are used to condition the space into a network of sights and systems (*associations* is the word Olson uses in her introduction) that together orchestrate an ecology of bodily sensations. The psychological term *automatism* refers to involuntary actions and processes that fall outside the control of the conscious mind, such as breathing or dreaming. *Cast of Mind* did not begin with preconceived notions of a finished product, but rather emerged from associations between space, object, and image. Olson choreographs the experience of architecture with devices of addition and subtraction, doubling and mirroring, and the (dis)assembly of openings and divisions that allow images to appear and disappear as in a dream. The result (and the condition, necessarily) is a durational experience of the environment: The audience must calibrate to the space over time, aware that what was previously there has been altered.

Through spatial twists and reconfigurations, the exhibition's early sense of constraint gives way to a controlled expansiveness. My mind goes to Marcel Duchamp's love of chess, to the humor and pleasure he found in destabilizing and distending the structure of the game. In chess, the value of each piece and its possible moves are derived from its relationship to other pieces. Olson's, too, is a game within the possible, of moving pieces into disorganized and reorganized placements, and seeking distinctions, amplifications, and differences within (through) a container. Without stability, there would be no instability. Boundaries are erotic. They force us to create from within a defined space, give us something to push up against.

The first hole emerged in April. *A small bore of light, but did it see her*, 2023, was a three-inch port between the two spaces, mouth and stomach. It punctured the introductory text in the small gallery and radiated light from the encased windows into the larger one, beckoning proximity, becoming larger as the months went by.

"Push-pull" theory refers to the tension created by contrasting forces: a dynamic of alternating cycles of closeness and withdrawal, intimacy and estrangement, or visual elements that appear to come forward or recede on the canvas (this latter effect is attributed to Hans Hofmann). *A small bore of light, but did it see her* is both protrusion and crevice, viewfinder and blinder, two- and three-dimensional, alluring and inaccessible. In the large gallery, it sits above the off-white mural *Reflective Comedy, standing shoulder wall*, 2023, which wraps around the four walls at Olson's shoulder height. The bodily register feels intimate, at odds with the hole's placement well above standard eye height. Our bodily perceptions are suddenly broken down by this scale shift, as if in a (dis)embodied twilight zone between dream and ordinary consciousness where logic and the relative values of size no longer correspond to reality.

Lining the stomach, an assembly of light fixtures titled *What I would be if I wasn't what I am, I, I*, n.d., hang evenly from lengthy suspension lines and create the illusion of a secondary drop ceiling cutting the gallery's height in half. The works are odd and menacing, acquiring a further amorphous quality as they slowly move toward the back of the gallery. Claws narrowing in on their prey. By the end of August, they've clustered around the back of the room to shine a spotlight onto the disassembled, partially replicated tabletop panels lying on the floor titled *Total Work (Rest)*, 2023: a dreamlike deformation produced by the memory of the table past.

In September, the previously walled-over windows were uncovered. *Sluice (A weird rewriting of negative capability?)*, 2023, was built to bisect the space, and Olson was asked if she had nightmares.

Gins and Arakawa again: "Start by thinking of architecture as a tentative constructing toward a holding in place. Architecture's holding in place occurs within and as part of a prevailing atmospheric condition that others routinely call biosphere, but which we, feeling the need to stress its dynamic nature, have renamed bioscleave."[5]

How does one begin to tentatively construct a holding in place? Tentative, elusive, a "tenuous event-fabric" or "event-matrix" made up of matter and all its internal energy.[6] "Who moves through this mass of chaos, this massive mix of order and chaos, has sites of awareness buried there within it."[7] The task involves attunement, a phenomenological reflexivity of the perceiving subject, but the bioscleave does not simply come to be as an untempered mood or projection; it also entails a *cleaving*, a severing, a forging, a cutting apart, or off, on the part of the architect.

The psychologist and psychophysicist Gustav Theodor Fechner developed the field of psychological aesthetics by relating physical stimuli to the contents of consciousness. These insights were crucial to the establishment of notions of space and atmosphere in art and architectural theory. For Fechner, atmosphere is the giant "breathing organ" shared by all forms of matter, the everyday experience of corporeal presence that is usually neglected by theorists of aesthetics.[8] Speaking of atmosphere means returning to a less intellectual and more material state of consciousness—something like the intoxicated dream-consciousness of the Surrealist state of mind, where, Benjamin writes, image takes precedence "not only before meaning. Also before the self."[9]

With the severing of the main gallery into halves, the yellow light softens around the arrangement of objects down below. There is a metal aperture recessed into the four-and-a-half-foot-high wall spanning the width of the main gallery, providing a viewpoint but not an entry into the cast of objects that make up *Total Work (Rest)*. The push-pull of this aperture/barrier changes the sculptural encounter, renders it photographic. You take in the work with your eyes, yes, but experience it in your body: in the vulnerability of feeling watched by an intrusive gaze, or seized from behind, as you peer at the forbidden objects beyond the half-wall. You are aware of where you are and of the direction in which you are facing, but your knowledge of the room's representative features (the elongated layout, tall ceilings) no longer corresponds to the vision before your eyes. The axis of *this* room, the room you are in, has shifted. In Olson's eerie removal of peripheral vision, you are unmoored. And you stand differently, aware of every part of your body and its now inhibited movement in space.

For a work of procedural architecture to succeed, per Gins and Arakawa, it must be conceived as a teeming ecosystem, in a cycle of constant sensing and adapting. There can be no finitude to the process of transformation. This is similar to Benjamin's dialectical image, which is never truly still but is buzzing with latent histories and future projections. *Cast of Mind* relies on the malleability of memory and vision to animate and reanimate its form, and this is a system of flows, which conjoin as atmosphere. The dream state is created in those conflicts of presence and absence where formal systems are seen to snap, crack open. Far from an ideal calm, the dream state conjured is a continuously shaping, uncanny non-site courting the limits of embodied experience itself.

Staring at the unhomeliness of Olson's Iteration X through my laptop screen, I think of Mike Kelley's heptaptych *The Poltergeist*, 1979, in which one panel reads: "Teen-age term 'dreamy' meaning beautiful. Beauty like the relaxed expression of one asleep. It makes sense that the adolescent is drawn to the beauty of the dreamer."[10] Beneath a drawing of two identical vases spinning on opposite axes, the text continues: "And is also susceptible to the Poltergeist. The dream state made material. One can become dreamy. Strange though, how the ideal dream state is calm; the actual—chaos."

Is that not a feeling of liberation?

NOTES

1. Thomas Metzinger, "Why Are Dreams Interesting for Philosophers? The Example of Minimal Phenomenal Selfhood, Plus an Agenda for Future Research," *Frontiers in Psychology* 4 (October 2013): 12.

2. Walter Benjamin, *The Arcades Project*, ed. Rolf Tiedmann, trans. Howard Eiland and Kevin McLaughlin (Cambridge, MA, and London: Belknap Press/Harvard University Press, 1999).

3. Christian Metz, "The Imaginary Signifier," *Screen* 16, no. 2 (Summer 1975): 14.

4. "Bioscleave House (Lifespan Extending Villa)," Arakawa + Gins Tokyo Office website, accessed March 5, 2025, https://www.architectural-body.com/?p=7147&lang=en.

5. Madeline Gins and Shusaku Arakawa, *Architectural Body* (Tuscaloosa: University of Alabama Press, 2002), 48.

6. Gins and Arakawa, *Architectural Body*, 48.

7. Gins and Arakawa, *Architectural Body*, 51.

8. Gustav Theodor Fechner, quoted in Ákos Moravánszky, "Architectures to Be Inhaled: Constructing the Ephemeral," in *The Death and Life of the Total Work of Art: Henry van de Velde and the Legacy of a Modern Concept*, ed. Carsten Ruhl, Chris Dähne, and Rixt Hoekstra (Berlin: JOVIS Verlag, 2017), 229.

9. Walter Benjamin, "Surrealism: The Last Snapshot of the European Intelligentsia," trans. Edmund Jephcott, *New Left Review* 108 (1978): 48.

10. Mike Kelley, *The Poltergeist*, 1979, framed photographic prints, 7 parts, overall dimensions variable.

Iteration IX

October 31–November 20, 2023

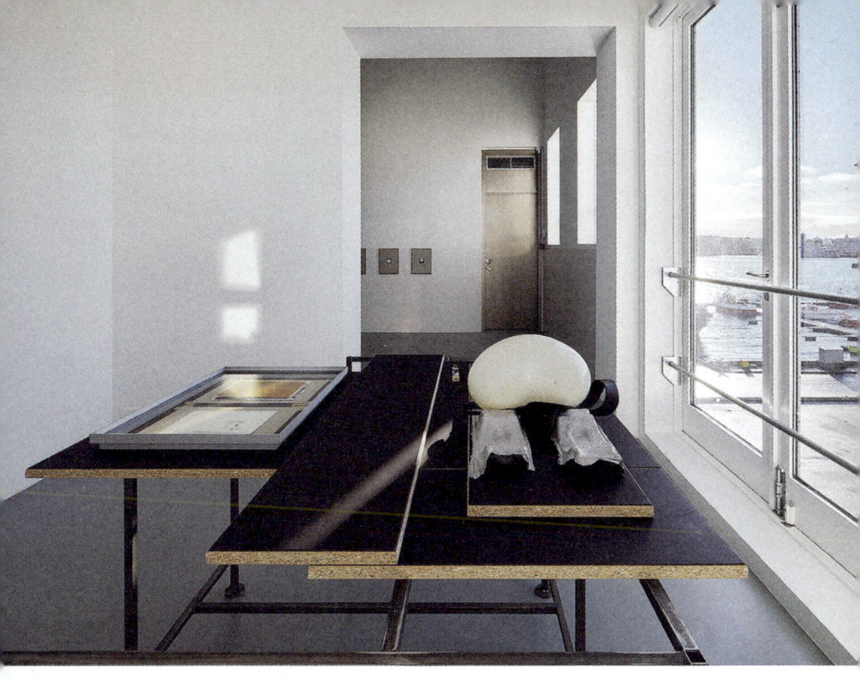

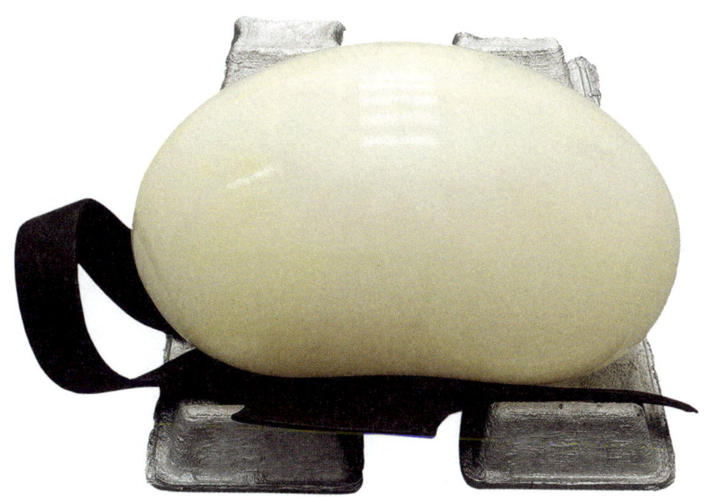

Clock / Painting (detail), 2023

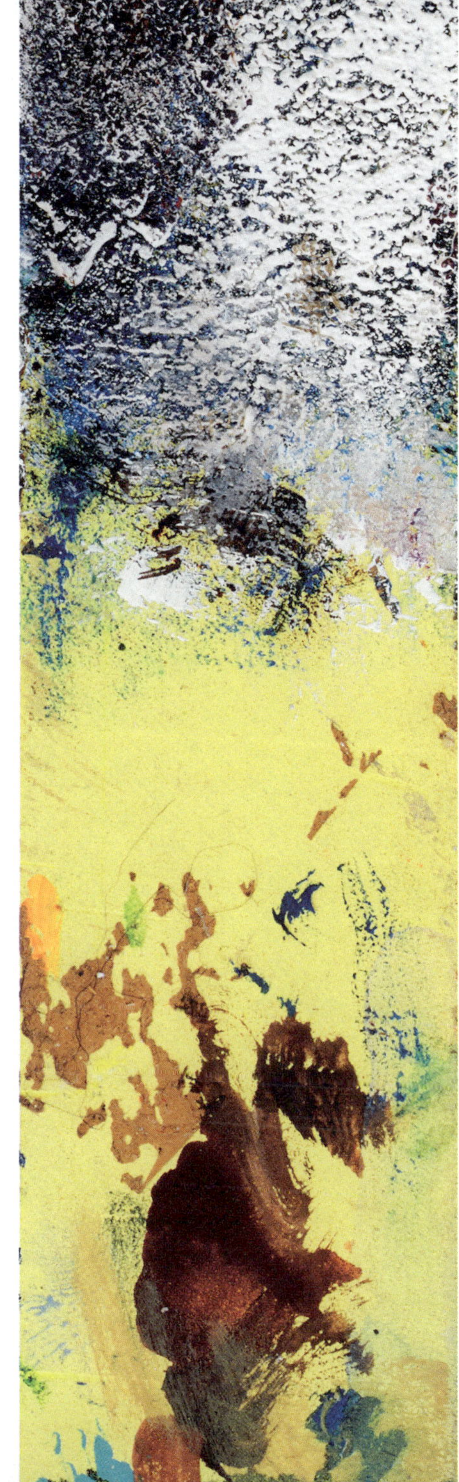

Artists Book (detail), 2010–23

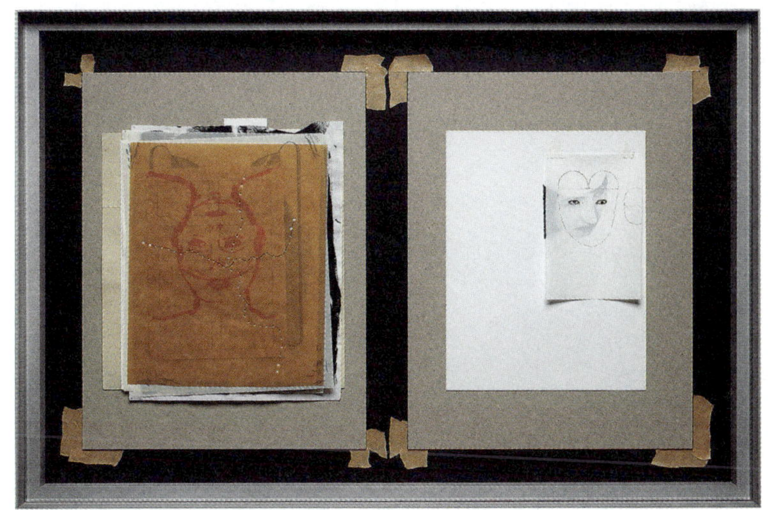

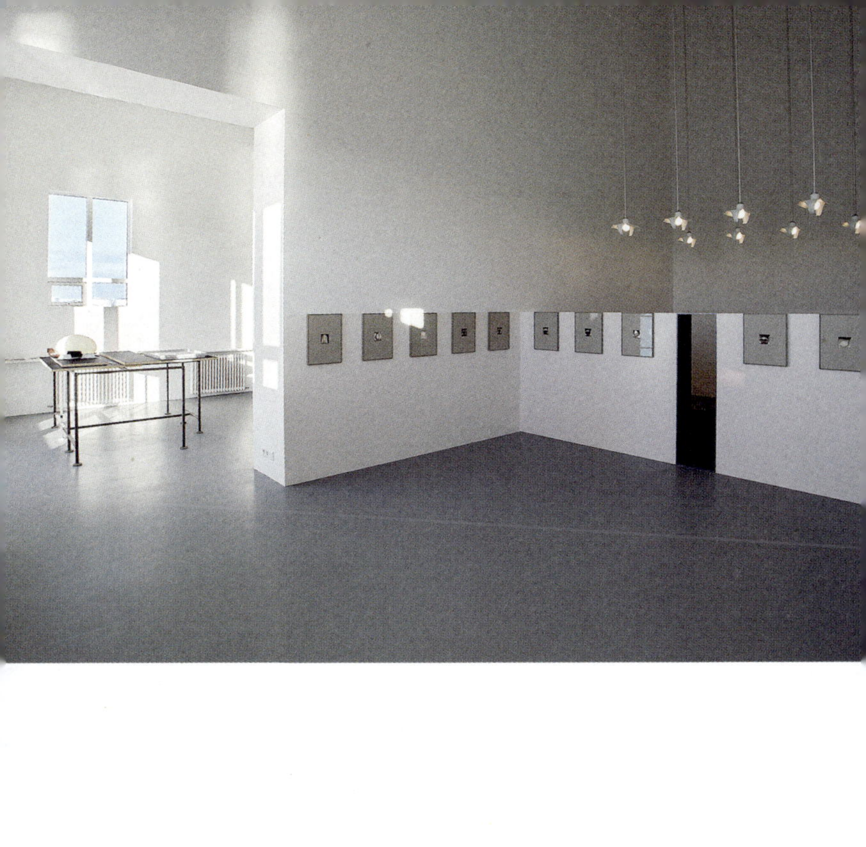

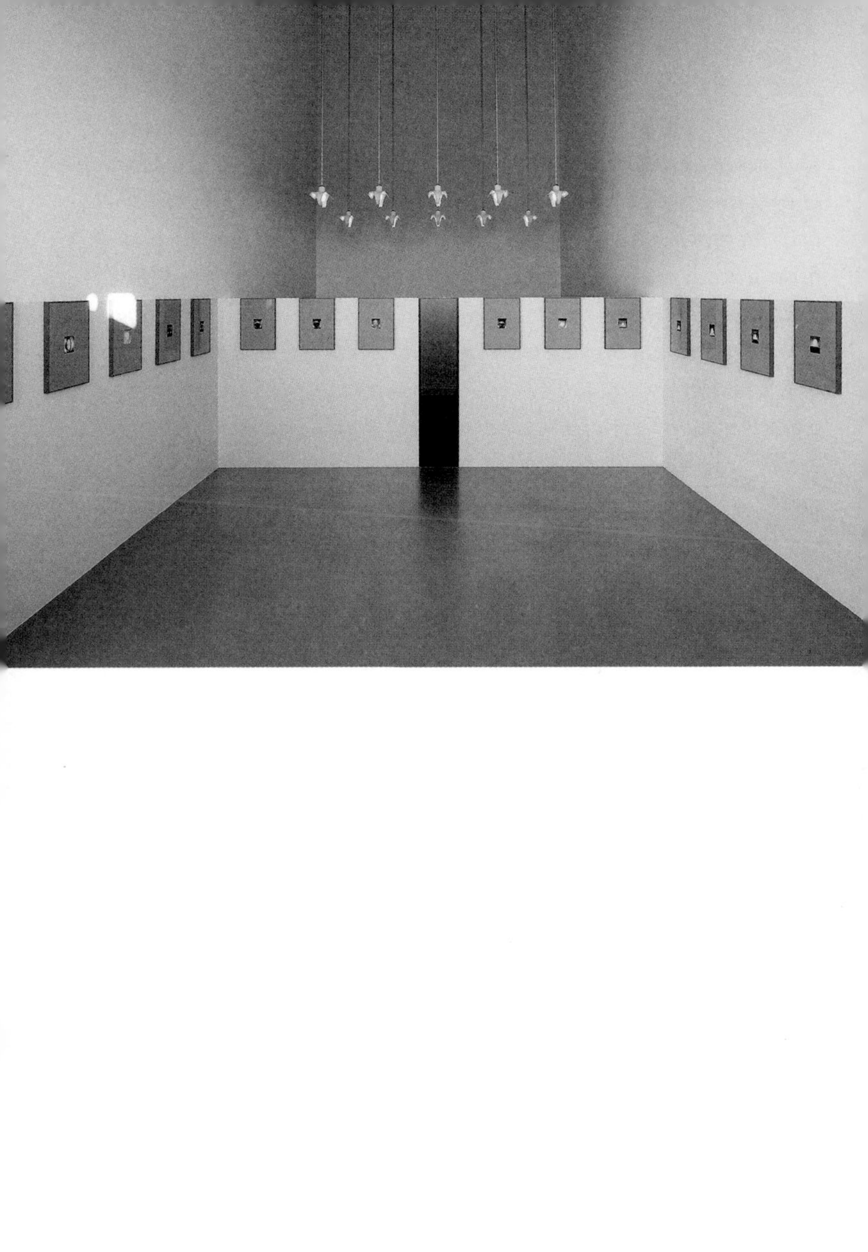

I was then a we, can it be that I am the subject, an actor, common plural fixed for a camera to which these rooms are now fit Ferocious battle with repetition, of others, the crumbs and dust, gathering ashes, adhesion of eggs, finally things in place for a moment Senses Visibly, but maybe half-life represented by the vast room means sitting in it not being in it because who could remove such a room from self From each end ends, plot, second language, treads herself an extenuating time luxuriating time infascinating time they watch her tread on, full forward and going nowhere very remarkable Do we need to open and shut the window when it is transparent from the start Or a special organ for what trickles through the hourglass? (details), 2021–23

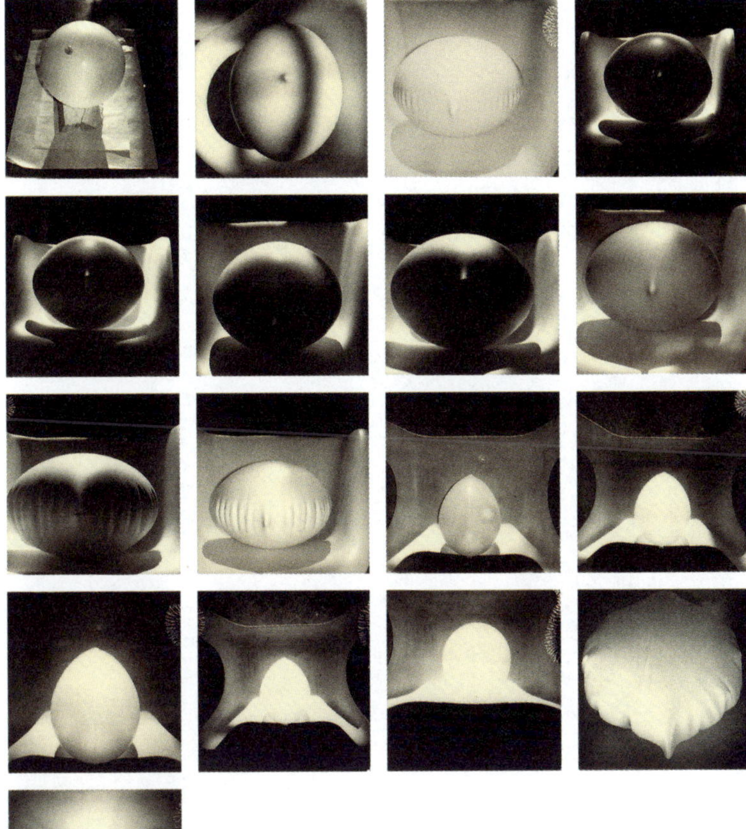

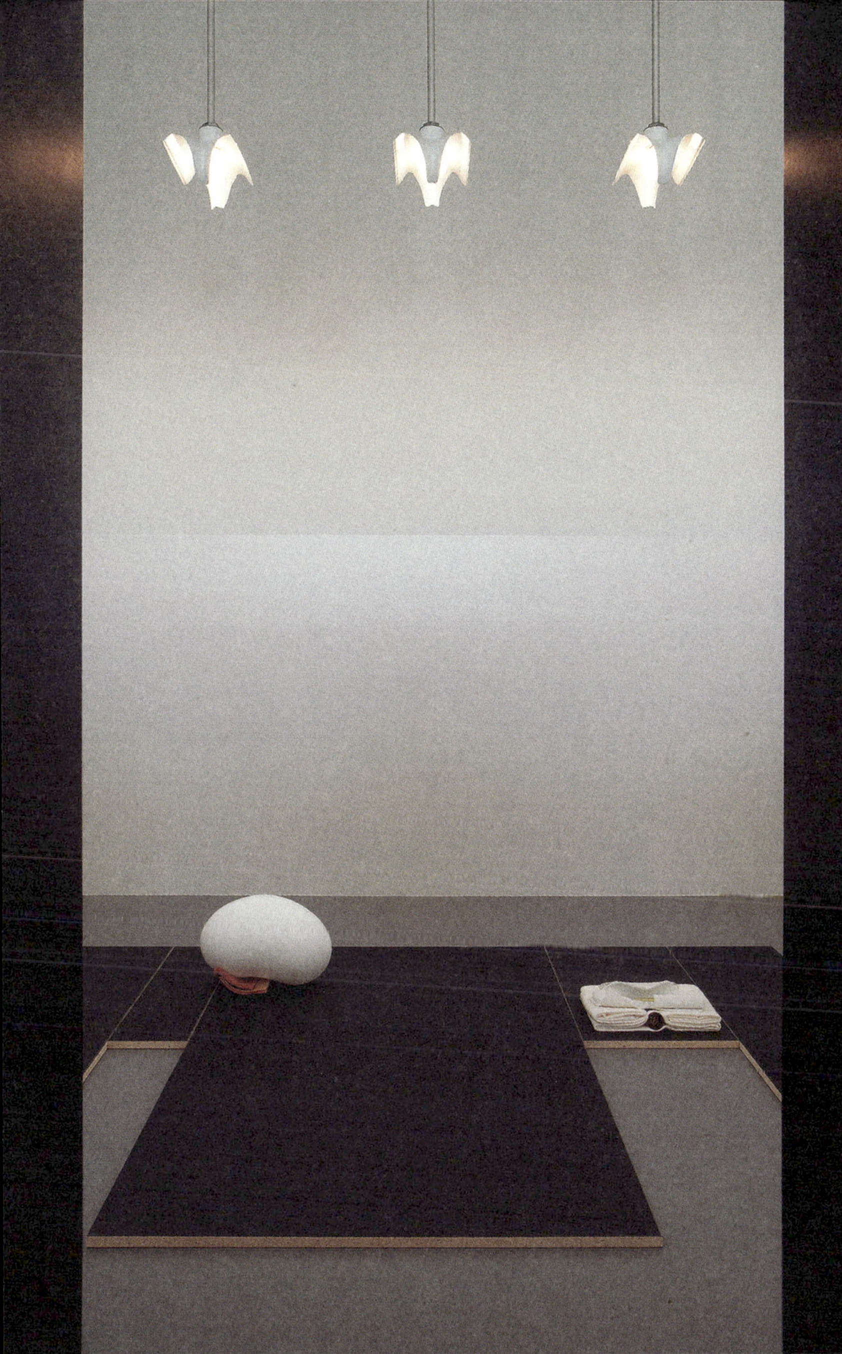

Clock / Painting (detail), 2023

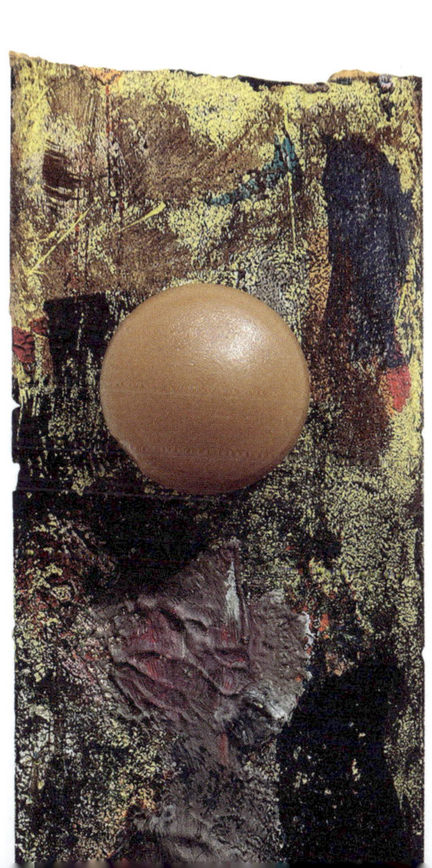

EXCERPTS FROM *THE END*

Aditi Machado

THE END—and now what? Am I changed? Is the world? I've lifted myself off the page and what sort of gesture is this? Isn't especially dramatic, it happens simply, and I mark it. Poems do end, at least materially.

THE END: "You must change your life."

I must change my life!

I must read the poem and change my life.

Hah.

BUT *is* that the poem's end?[1] I re-read and now it says something like *you must, at all times, endlessly change your life. You cannot not change your life.*

The poem is Rainer Maria Rilke's "Archaic Torso of Apollo" in the English translation by Stephen Mitchell. In it a grand sculpture of the Greek god Apollo stands before the eyes—grander, it would seem, and more ruinously beautiful for its lack of head, arms, and legs. "We cannot know," the poem begins. "We cannot know his legendary head / with eyes like ripening fruit."

That is to say, we begin not-knowing. The absent head confronts us and names us in our unknowing. How should we look upon this headless thing, "we" who have heads? The torso is so big, it is as though our heads are atilt, studying the empty space above the severed neck and chiseling into it the impossible eyes looking back at us.

> We cannot know his legendary head
> with eyes like ripening fruit. And yet his torso
> is still suffused with brilliance from inside,
> like a lamp, in which his gaze, now turned to low,
>
> gleams in all its power....

Compressed in Apollo's torso lie the features of his missing head. A gaze materializes in it; there is a smile in the musculature around the genitals, and everywhere radiant hair. Everything is getting magnified. The stone isn't simply gleaming, it's "burst[ing] like a star" "from all the borders of itself"—the torso is erupting out of its own material and the dim gaze that once was now gleams multiply out of multiple eyes: "there is no place / that does not see you." In the demotic, *you feel so seen.*

You must change your life.

AN "OTHER ECONOMY": Lyn Hejinian's "The Rejection of Closure" is an argument for the "open text" which does not provide closure, is open to readerly participation (i.e., making or *poesis*) and hermeneutic multiplicity, and "resists the cultural tendencies that seek to identify and fix material and turn it into a product; that is, it resists reduction and commodification." Hejinian finds that the "open text" engages in an alternative economy as described by Luce Irigaray: an economy that "diverts the linearity of a project, undermines the target-object of desire, explodes the polarization of desire on only one pleasure, and disconcerts fidelity to only one discourse."

THE EPIPHANY, WHATEVER THAT IS: An Incomplete Inventory:

- When I walk home from the bus stop, I sometimes have an epiphany about an event earlier in the day, how better to answer a student's question or how to fix my essay. A cartoon lightbulb floats above my head.
- Reality TV contestants not only have epiphanies but stylized formulae for delivering them in the filmed confessional.
- On social media, epiphanies arrive with the speed of self-help and in electronic bluster.
- In the oft cinematized narratives of personal success, epiphanies are stepping stones to self-actualization.
- In some Christian sects, Epiphany is a religious feast celebrating the manifestation of Christ as son of their god. It is the corporeal revelation of a theological truth.
- The Greek verb *epiphanein* means something like "to come suddenly into view."
- In modernist fiction, "the epiphany signifies a moment of clarity in which artistic or ontological truths are exposed," writes Maria-Daniella Dick.
- In contemporary United-Statesian poetry, epiphany is typically associated with closure or resolution at the end of a poem. In the preface to her critical essay "The Rejection of Closure," Hejinian offers as a "negative model" of closure the "coercive, epiphanic mode in some contemporary lyric poetry … with its smug pretension to universality and its tendency to cast the poet as guardian to Truth."
- But if I remove from epiphany the expectation that it offer closure, I begin to conceive of it, simply, as an aspect of the procedures of language. A kind of thickening up, a tendency toward music or noise, an opening out. In that

moment it feels like something is being made manifest—a corporeal revelation of some kind of (not capital T) truth. It's the "coming suddenly into view" of an elucidation. And as with coming into view of, say, a feature of the landscape when one is driving toward it, past it, ahead of it, one might move toward *and* away from the epiphany without it necessarily becoming the *fact* of the poem. The *thing* for which you remember it, if you remember it at all.

NOTE

1. End as a boundary in space and time, but also end as purpose.

Iteration X

November 21–December 20, 2023

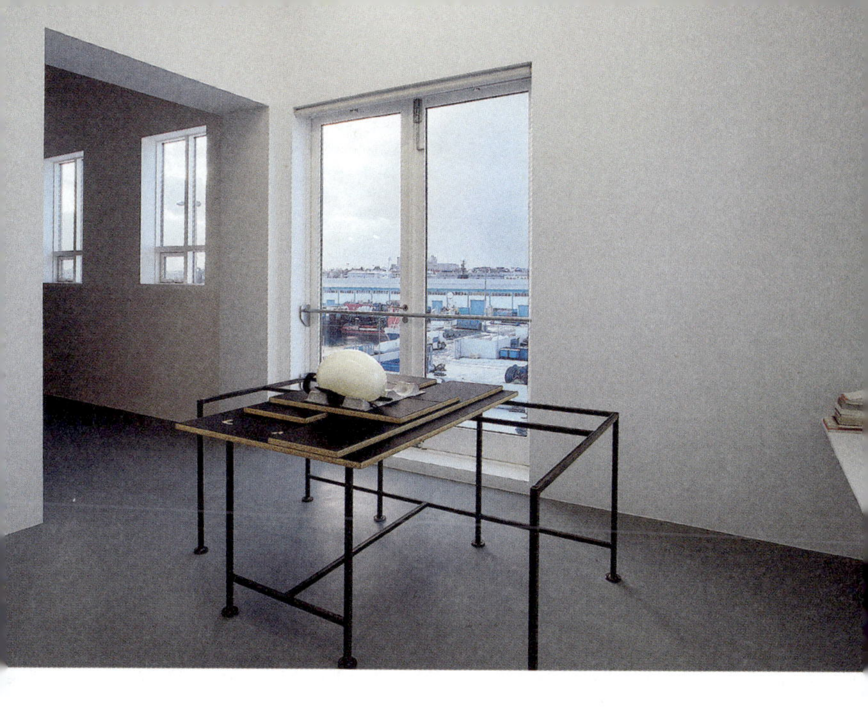

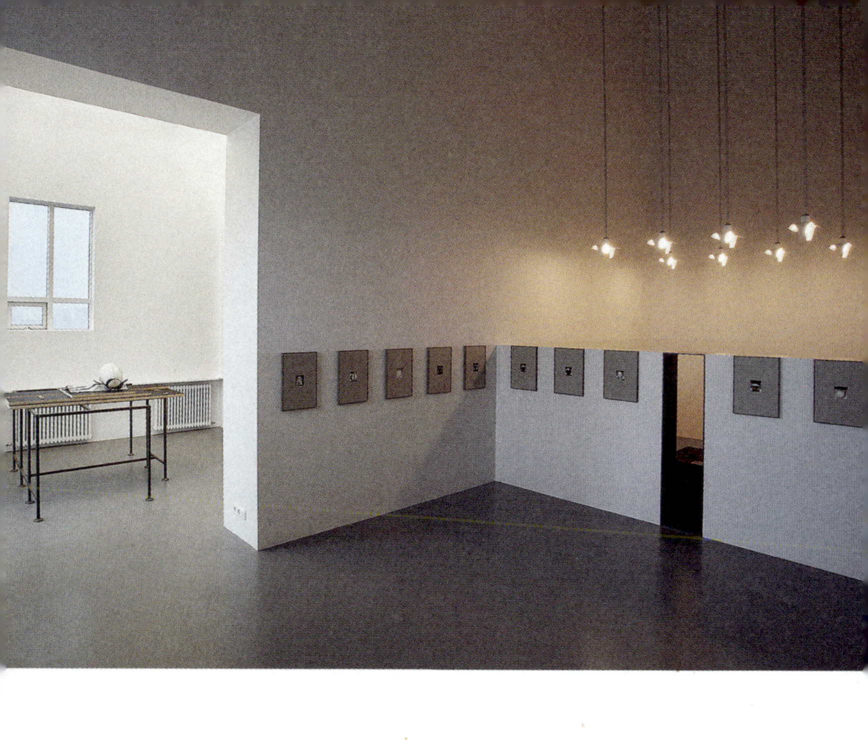

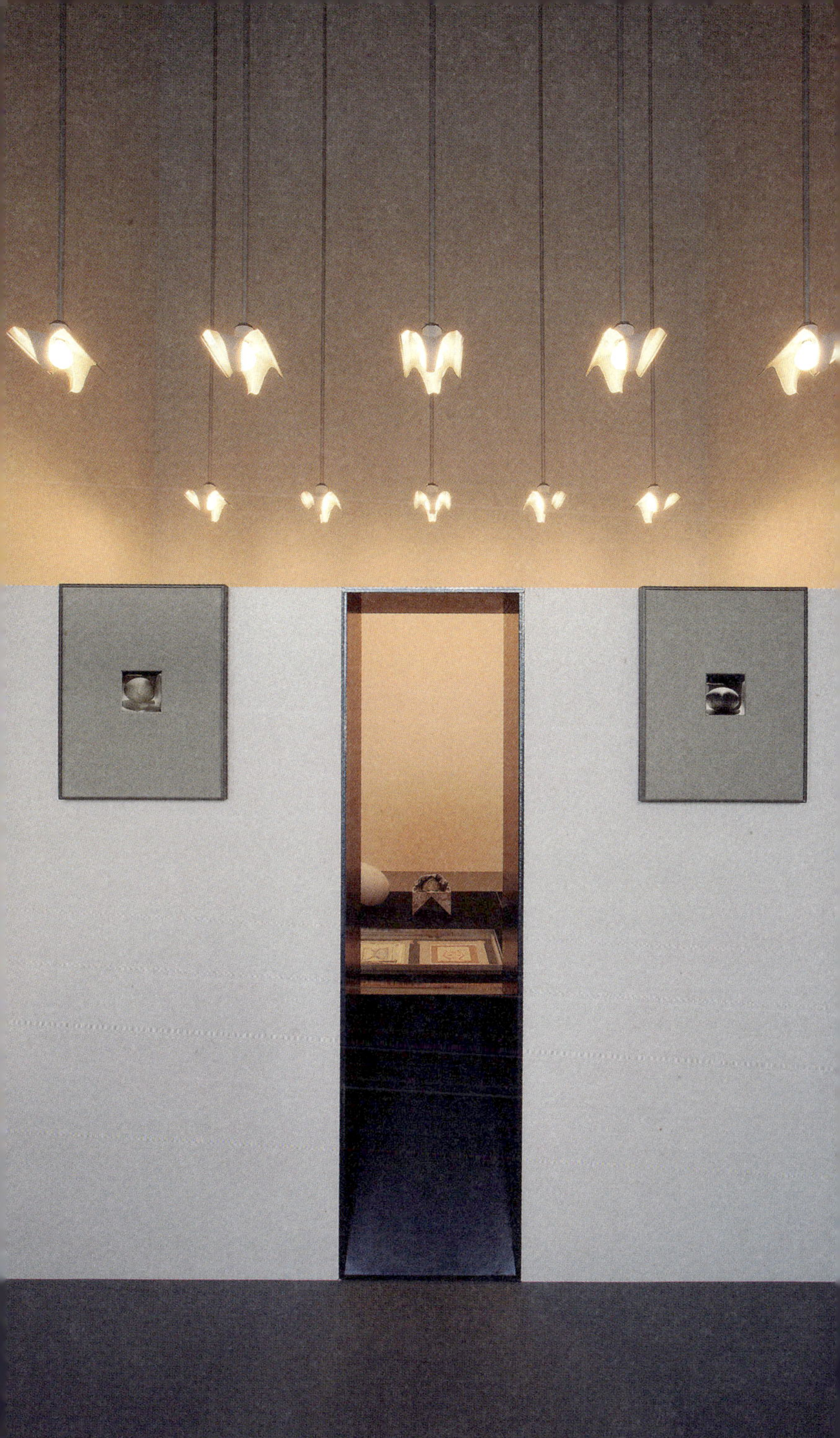

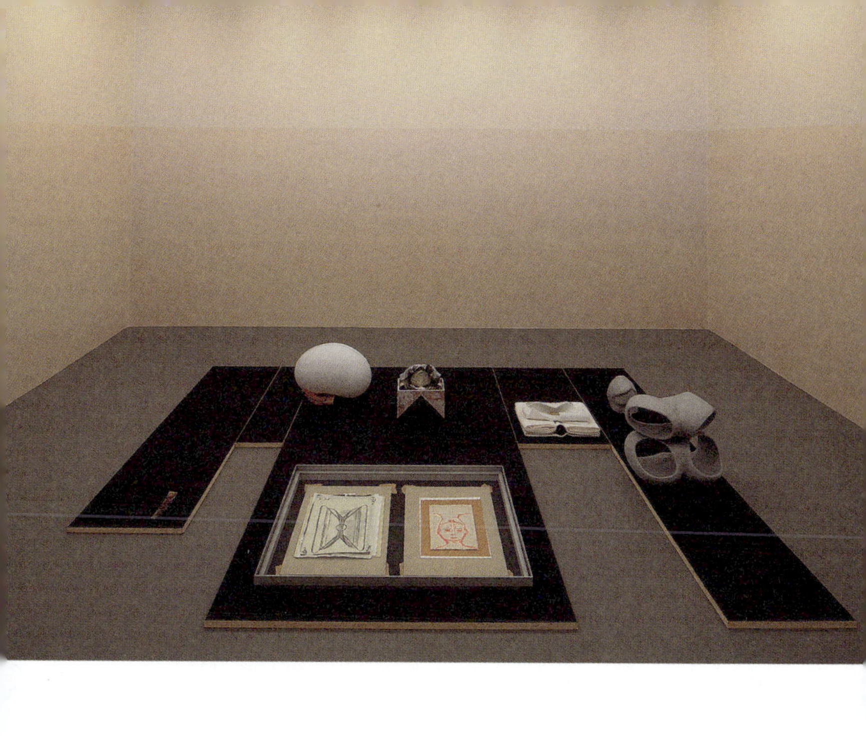

Clock / Painting (detail), 2023

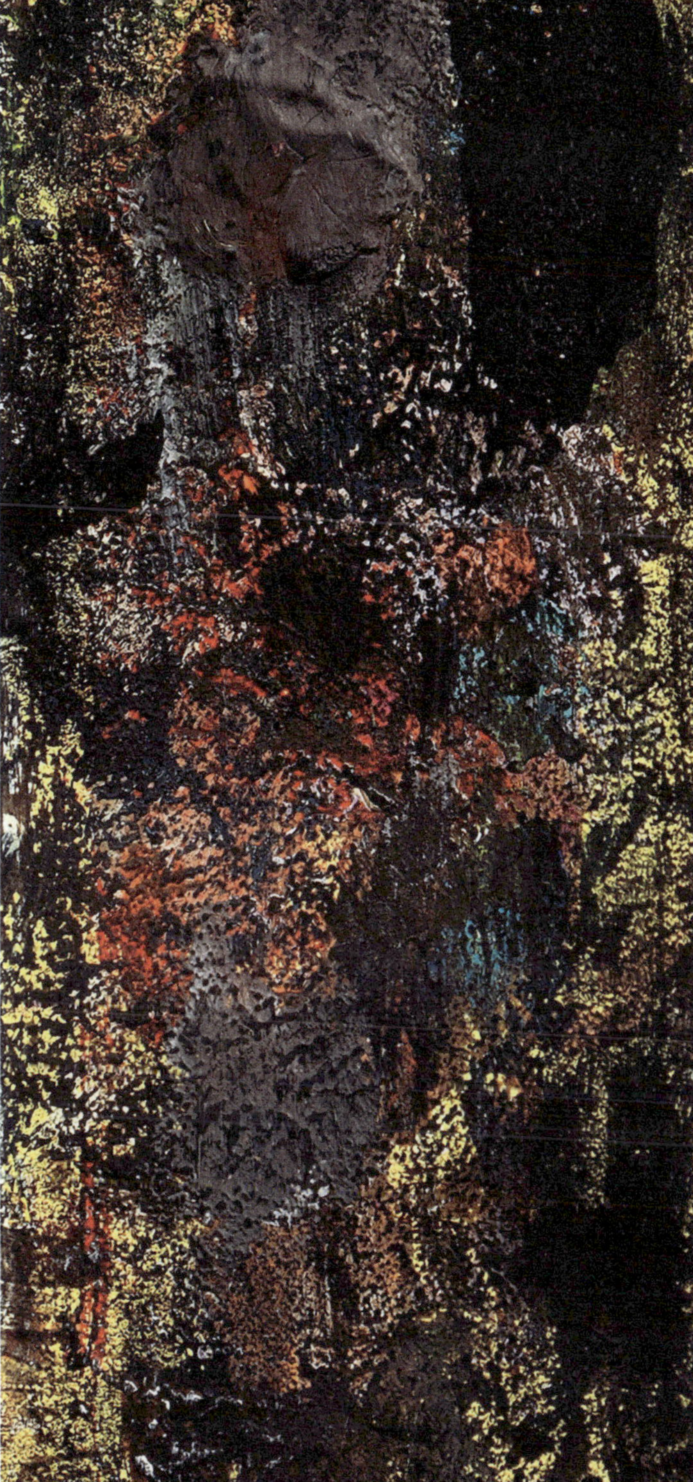

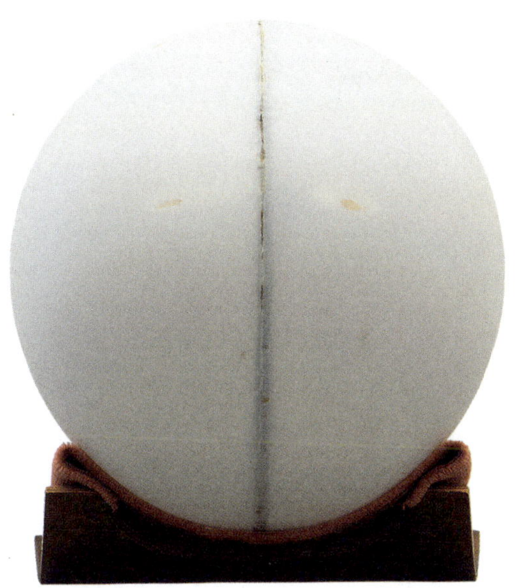

Feminine Thought, model, 2022–23

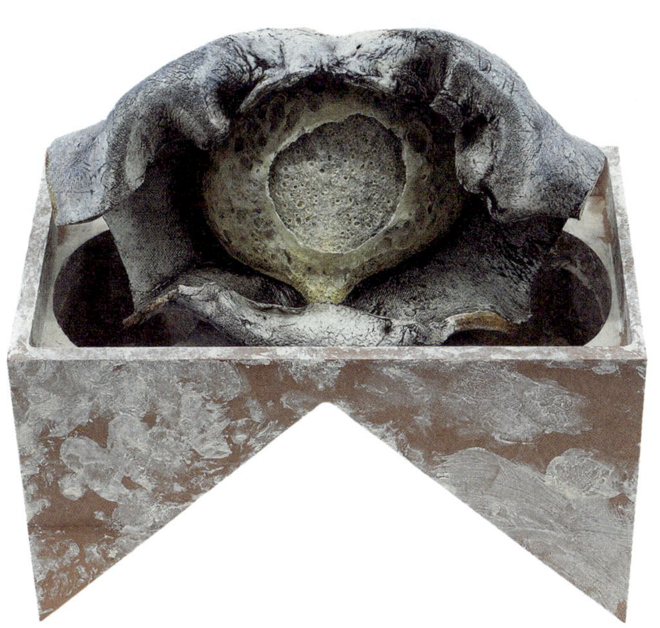

Artists Book (detail), 2010–23

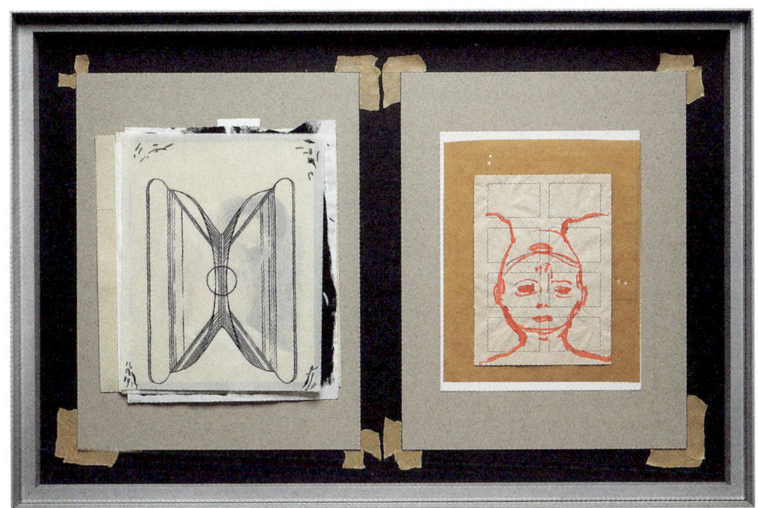

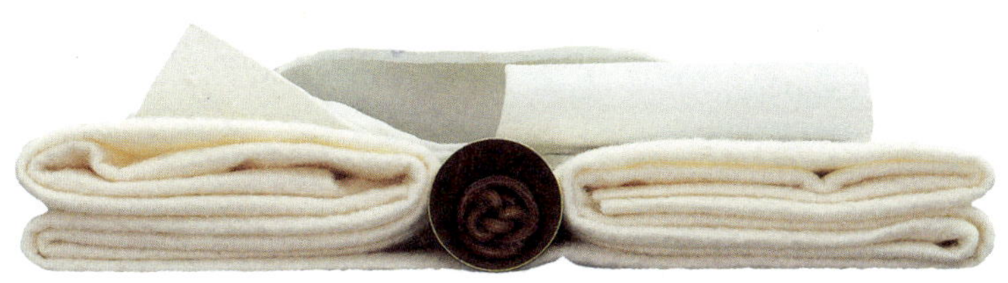

Body Parsed, Three Rooms, 2018

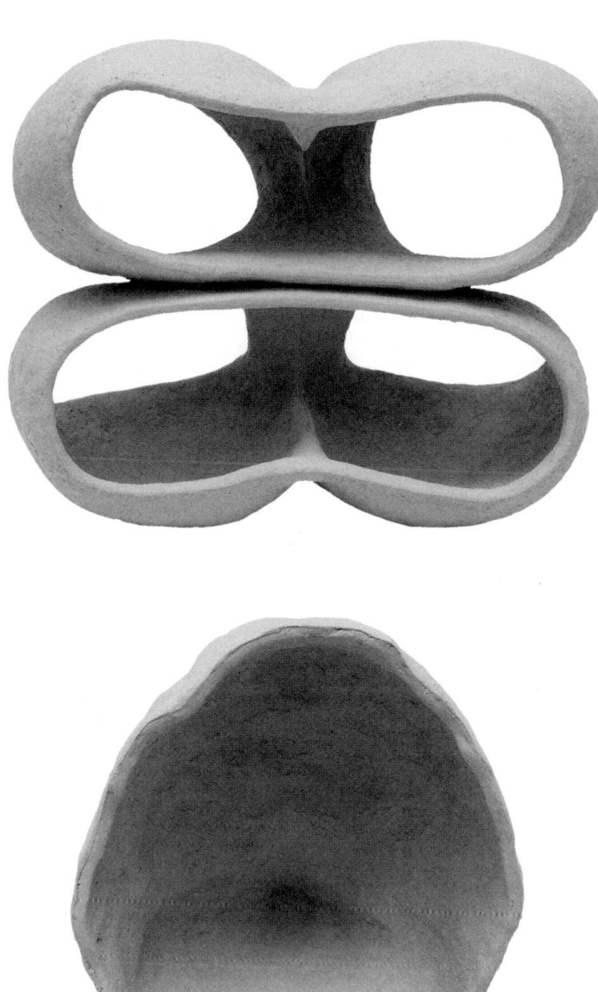

INDEX OF WORKS

A Feminine Thought (1934–2021), 2021–22
Inkjet print and UV-printed matboard in powder-coated aluminum frame
20 × 13 ¾ × 1 in. (51.5 × 35.5 × 2.5 cm)
Iteration I
pp. 13, 15, 17

A small bore of light, but did it see her, 2023
Hole in a wall with a concealed window
Overall dimensions variable
Iterations IV, V, VI
pp. 137, 139, 141, 143, 175, 183, 217, 223

Architect's Mouth, 2022
Glazed porcelain, acrylic paint, milk paint, epoxy, found metal drawer pull
4 × 3 ½ × 2 in. (10.1 × 8.9 × 5 cm)
Iterations I, II
pp. 37, 39, 75

Artists Book, 2010–23
Aluminum, glass, binder's board; including *Reflective Comedy [Apology]*, 2016, ink, graphite, gouache on two pieces of paper; *Copy Drawing*, 2010, adhesive label, ink and photocopy on paper; *Drawing for doubled self, building draft*, 2011, ink on paper; *Overlay*, 2018, permanent ink on paper; *Reflective Comedy*, 2017, graphite, gouache, aluminum tape, silver gelatin prints, staple, tracing paper; *Vertical Drawing*, 2013, ink and offset on paper; *History Mother Little Sister, draft*, 2020; ink on vellum; *Reflective Comedy (1986)*, 2016, gouache, graphite on dust jacket; *Drawing for What I would be if I wasn't what I am*, 2022, ink on vellum; *Horizontal Drawing*, 2013, ink and offset on paper; *History Mother Little Sister*, 2022, graphite on punctured paper; *Self as Gray, with Mask*, 2018–23, ink and tape on paper and vellum

2 × 30 × 20 in. (5.1 × 76.2 × 50.8 cm)
Iterations IV, V, VI, VII, VIII, IX, X
pp. 123, 133, 137, 151, 155, 171, 175, 179, 193, 209, 217, 221, 231, 247, 251, 257, 281, 285, 289, 315, 321, 351, 359

Below and Throw, 2020–21
Inkjet print and UV-printed matboard in powder-coated aluminum frame
11 × 15 × 1 in. (28 × 38.1 × 2.5 cm)
Iteration III
pp. 93, 97, 101

Body Parsed, Three Rooms, 2018
Modeling clay, epoxy putty, acrylic, aluminum panel
39 × 24 × 19 in. (99 × 61 × 48.3 cm)
Iterations II, X
pp. 61, 65, 69, 79, 351, 363

Camera (am I disorganized because I lost something I didn't need?), 2020–22
Polycarbonate sheet, MDF, screws, stainless steel, acrylic ink, staples, offset prints, silver gelatin prints, inkjet prints, paper, acetate, fabric, latex paint
26 ½ × 60 ½ × 10 in. (67.3 × 153.7 × 25.4 cm)
Iterations IV, V, VI
pp. 143, 147, 183, 185, 225

Clock / Painting, 2023
Gouache on paper, pin
1 × 4 × ½ in. (2.5 × 10.2 × 1.3 cm)
Iterations IV, V, VI, VII, VIII, IX, X
pp. 123, 131, 171, 173, 209, 247, 301, 331, 351, 353

Clock / Painting, 2023
Gouache on paper, pin
1 × 8 × ½ in. (2.5 × 20.3 × 1.3 cm)
Iterations VIII, IX, X
pp. 281, 287, 289, 315, 319, 345

Coming in with your back turned, 2021–22
Inkjet print and UV-printed matboard in powder-coated aluminum frame
29 × 19 ¼ × 1 ¼ in. (73.7 × 48.8 × 3.2 cm)
Iterations II, III
pp. 71, 73, 107

Endless House, plastic drawing, 2017
PVA size, acrylic, vinyl paint and sand on polyurethane foam
7 × 10 × 10 in. (17.8 × 25.4 × 25.4 cm)
Iteration III
pp. 109, 111

Feminine Thought, model, 2022–23
Glazed porcelain, unfired porcelain, polyurethane modeling board
9 × 8 ½ × 5 ¼ in. (22.5 × 21.5 × 13 cm)
Iterations I, III, X
pp. 13, 15, 19, 25, 93, 97, 99, 103, 349, 351, 357

Forehead and Brain, 2018
PVA size, oil stick, polyurethane foam
4 × 9 ¾ × 3 in. (10.2 × 24.7 × 7.6 cm)
Iterations VI, VII, VIII
pp. 211, 213, 247, 255, 281

I was then a we, can it be that I am the subject, an actor, common plural fixed for a camera to which these rooms are now fit Ferocious battle with repetition, of others, the crumbs and dust, gathering ashes, adhesion

of eggs, finally things in place for a moment Senses Visibly, but maybe half-life represented by the vast room means sitting in it not being in it because who could remove such a room from self From each end ends, plot, second language, treads herself an extenuating time luxuriating time infascinating time they watch her tread on, full forward and going nowhere very remarkable Do we need to open and shut the window when it is transparent from the start Or a special organ for what trickles through the hourglass?, 2021–23
Internal dye diffusion transfer prints, binder's board, powder-coated aluminum frames
17 parts, each 16 × 12 ¼ in. (40.6 × 31.1 cm), overall dimensions variable
Iterations IX, X
pp. 323, 325, 327, 347, 349

Introductions by Kate Zambreno, 2018/2023
Vinyl on a wall with a concealed window
Overall dimensions variable
Iterations I, II, III, IV, V, VI
pp. 23, 25, 67, 69, 103, 105, 135, 137, 139, 175, 217

Liar's Envelope, 2020–23
Glazed porcelain, paper, gouache, cotton, celluloid, brass, epoxy glue, silicone
3 × 13 × 9 in. (7.6 × 33 × 23 cm)
Iterations IV, V, VI, VII, IX, X
pp. 123, 129, 171, 173, 209, 219, 247, 253, 257, 329, 351, 361

Plen, cycle, 2022–23
Steel, parabolic reflector, eggshell, glazed porcelain
17 × 16 × 17 in. (42.2 × 40.6 × 43.2)
Iterations IV, V, VI, VII
pp. 143, 145, 187, 189, 223, 259, 261, 269

Reflective Comedy, standing shoulder wall, 2023
Glossy latex paint on all walls within one room
Overall dimensions variable
Iterations VII, VIII, IX, X
pp. 259, 261, 263, 291, 293, 301, 323, 325, 329, 347, 351

Rifted Grid, per fluid, 2021–22
Inkjet print and UV-printed matboard in powder-coated aluminum frame
24 ½ × 16 × 1 ¼ in. (62.2 × 40.6 × 3.2 cm)
Iteration II
pp. 61, 63

Round Room (present/present), 2022
Plexiglass, dye-sublimation print on aluminum, silicone
58 × 46 × 1 in. (147.3 × 116.8 × 2.5 cm)
Iteration VIII
pp. 293, 297

Sluice (A weird rewriting of negative capability?), 2023
Drywall, latex paint, poplar, steel
Steel aperture 54 × 13 ¾ × 11 ¾ in. (137 × 35 × 30 cm), overall dimensions variable
Iterations VIII, IX, X
pp. 291, 293, 295, 299, 323, 325, 329, 347, 349

Spark steel or flint, oil, glass, delay, 2017–20
Inkjet print and UV-printed matboard in powder-coated aluminum frame
11 ½ × 24 × 1 ¼ in. (29.2 × 61 × 3.2 cm)
Iteration I
pp. 27, 33, 35

Standing Picture (present/present), 2021
Dye sublimation print on aluminum, silicone, plexiglass
32 × 36 × 1 in. (81.3 × 91.4 × 2.5 cm)
Iteration VII
pp. 259, 261, 267

Subject Position, 2022–23
Epoxy putty, epoxy resin, fiberglass, velvet, plywood
10 × 14 × 8 in. (25.4 × 35.6 × 20.3 cm)
Iterations IV, V, VI, VII, VIII, IX, X
pp. 123, 127, 137, 171, 175, 177, 209, 217, 259, 261, 299, 301, 329, 349, 351, 355

Subject Position, I, I, 2022–23
Epoxy resin, fiberglass, aluminum cast, leather
12 × 18 × 22 in. (30.5 × 45.7 × 55.9 cm)
Iterations VIII, IX, X
pp. 281, 283, 289, 315, 317, 345

Total Work (Cast of Mind), 2023
Steel, particle board, linoleum, glue, screws, impermanent inclusions
34 × 63 × 90 in. (86.5 × 160 × 228 cm)
Iterations I, II, III, IV, V, VI, VII, VIII, IX, X
pp. 13, 15, 21, 25, 27, 61, 69, 71, 93, 97, 103, 123, 137, 171, 173, 175, 209, 217, 223, 247, 249, 257, 259, 281, 289, 291, 315, 323, 345, 347

Total Work (Rest), 2023
Particle board, linoleum, glue, impermanent inclusions
5 parts, overall dimensions variable
Iterations VII, VIII, IX, X
pp. 259, 261, 265, 299, 301, 329, 349, 351

Umbra (Back of Head 01), 2021
Internal dye diffusion transfer print, binder's board, powder-coated aluminum frame
16 × 12 ¼ × 1 in. (40.6 × 31.1 × 2.5 cm)
Iteration V
pp. 171, 181, 183

Umbra (Etui 03), 2021
Internal dye diffusion transfer print, binder's board, powder-coated aluminum frame
16 × 12 ¼ × 1 in. (40.6 × 31.1 × 2.5 cm)
Iterations IV, VI
pp. 123, 125, 209, 211, 215

Underpinning, a twitch of glass, a pinch in the cloth, 2019–20
Inkjet print and UV-printed matboard in powder-coated aluminum frame
25 × 16 ½ × 1 ¼ in. (63.5 × 41.9 × 3.2 cm)
Iteration III
pp. 93, 95

What I would be if I wasn't what I am, I, I, n.d.
Stamped steel, powder coating, light socket and fitting, electrical wiring, light bulbs, aluminum conduit
10 parts, each 12 ¼ × 9 × 10 in. (31.1 × 22.9 × 25.4 cm), overall dimensions variable
Iterations I, II, III, IV, V, VI, VII, VIII, IX, X
pp. 27, 29, 35, 37, 71, 93, 107, 109, 143, 189, 223, 227, 259, 261, 291, 293, 299, 301, 323, 325, 329, 347, 349

CONTRIBUTORS

NUAR ALSADIR is a writer and psychoanalyst. She is the author of *Animal Joy: A Book of Laughter and Resuscitation* (2022) and the poetry collections *Fourth Person Singular* (2017) and *More Shadow than Bird* (2012). She is a fellow of the New York Institute for the Humanities and a member of the curatorial board of the Racial Imaginary Institute.

THOMAS DUNCAN is a doctoral candidate in the Department of Art History at the University of California, Los Angeles, where he is completing his dissertation, "'Exactly Wrong': Failure and Relationality in Andy Warhol's Polaroids, 1969–1978." His essays have appeared in publications including *May Revue*, *Flash Art*, and *Contemporary Art Review Los Angeles*.

MARIANA FERNÁNDEZ is a writer and independent curator who focuses on performance and visual art. Her writings have appeared in *Artforum*, *ArtReview*, *BOMB*, *e-flux Criticism*, *frieze*, *Momus*, and *X-TRA Contemporary Art Quarterly*, and in various exhibition catalogues. She is based in New York and Mexico City.

ADITI MACHADO is an author whose publications include the poetry collections *Material Witness* (2024), *Emporium* (2020), and *Some Beheadings* (2017). Her essay pamphlet *The End* (2020) discusses the ends of poetry and the ends of time.

SAWAKO NAKAYASU is a writer whose books include *Pink Waves* (2023), *Say Translation Is Art* (2020), and *Some Girls Walk into the Country They Are From* (2020). She teaches in the Literary Arts Department at Brown University.

KATE NESIN is a curator-at-large at the Art Institute of Chicago, where she has organized exhibitions of the work of Helena Almeida, Lucy McKenzie, Frances Stark, and Kemang Wa Lehulere, among others. She often writes about sculpture, recently in essays on Lutz Bacher, Nairy Baghramian, and Eva Hesse.

B. INGRID OLSON is an artist based in Chicago. Solo exhibitions of her work have been held at venues including Midway Contemporary Art, Minneapolis, Minnesota; Kunstverein Braunschweig, Braunschweig, Germany; fluent, Santander, Spain; Carpenter Center for the Visual Arts, Cambridge, Massachusetts; Secession, Vienna, Austria; and Buffalo AKG Art Museum, Buffalo, New York.

TH. KILLIAN ROACH is an artist based in New York and Los Angeles.

LESLIE MEREDITH WILSON is a writer on photography and the academic curator and director of research programs at the Art Institute of Chicago, where she collaborated on *David Goldblatt: No Ulterior Motive* in 2023. For Aperture, she organized the exhibition *The True America: Photographs by Ernest Cole*, currently touring.

KATE ZAMBRENO is a writer whose numerous books include *Animal Stories* (2025), *The Light Room* (2023), *Tone* (2023, coauthored with Sofia Samatar), *To Write as if Already Dead* (2021), *Drifts* (2020), and *Appendix Project: Talks and Essays* (2019). They are currently a doctoral candidate in Performance Studies at New York University.

ACKNOWLEDGMENTS

This book would not be without Chad Kloepfer. I would like to extend the deepest gratitude for this second collaboration and for your friendship. I continue to relish your insight, sensitivity, and solutions to problems that are perfectly synced but so unexpected.

Thank you to Karen Kelly and Barbara Schroeder for shaping and shepherding this publication. The nebulous, inclusive, and transformative way of thinking, and making, that happened within this exhibition and book could not feel more at home than with Dancing Foxes Press.

To Lucy Flint for your attention, patience, and guidance in editing a second book of mine—and also for teaching me the phrase that titled this show and book.

Also to Polly Watson for lending your fine-tooth comb, I thank you for your proofreading.

Thomas Duncan, Mariana Fernández, Kate Nesin, Th. Killian Roach, Leslie Meredith Wilson, and Kate Zambreno, I am honored to be in continued conversation with each of you. Thank you for your probing explorations of this project's various components, helping to make visible some parts of this complicated clock.

I am grateful to Nuar Alsadir, Aditi Machado, and Sawako Nakayasu for allowing me to excerpt your previous writing, grafting it so visibly onto this new situation so that our separate images now sit parallel here.

I would like to acknowledge Börkur Arnarson and Geneva Viralam for an invitation of the rarest variety. *Cast of Mind* was the most transformative experience I have had making an exhibition—to not only be allowed, but encouraged, to spread out, to rethink existing works, to experiment, to try to fail, and to change my thinking over the course of an entire year. The gratitude I feel is ineffable.

I extend this appreciation also to the rest of the team at i8 Gallery for their marathon of support throughout the process: Sigrún Birna Dagbjartsdóttir, Hrafnkell Guðmundsson, Dorothea Olesen Halldórsdóttir, Birkir Karlsson, and Eva Lín Vilhjálmsdóttir.

I thank all of those involved with making various components of the installation possible—printing, metalwork, milling fabrication, electrical work, wall painting, vinyl application, and the architectural adjustments—each for their time, skill, and expertise: Dan Gulick, Rúnar Guðnason, Kazuki Guzman, Heimisson, Sigurður Kárason, Elmar Freyr Kristjánsson, Latitude Chicago, Nikulás Stefán Nikulásson, Ásmundur Hrafn Sturluson, José Taymani, Sævar Smári Þórðarson, and Þorsteinn Viðarsson.

For the Sisyphean task of documenting the show with exacting accuracy ten times over, thank you to Vigfús Birgisson and Magnús Óli, with support from Hrafnkell Guðmundsson and Sam Stevens.

For loaning *Forehead and Brain*, thanks to Sigurður Gísli Pálmason.

I also want to acknowledge the books that were placed on the table within the exhibition, which played a significant part in shaping my headspace throughout its duration: *The Eyes of the Skin: Architecture and the Senses* by Juhani Pallasmaa, *Occasional Work and Seven Walks from the Office for Soft Architecture* by Lisa Robertson, *Plans for Sentences* by Renee Gladman, *Labyrinths* by Jorge Luis Borges, *Glyph* by Percival Everett, *Driven to Abstraction* by Rosmarie Waldrop, *Architectural Body* by Madeline Gins and Shusaku Arakawa, *The Missing Pieces* by Henri Lefebvre, *An Apartment on Uranus* by Paul B. Preciado, *ABC of Impossibility* by Simon Critchley, and *Nelly's Version* by Eva Figes.

For our exchanges that helped shape this show, thank you to Dan Byers, Alex Chitty, Jenny Harris, Christine Mehring, Meg Onli, Noah Singer, and Constantin Thun.

Always to John. As ever, more and more, I appreciate you.

— B. Ingrid Olson

COLOPHON

This book was produced in conjunction with *Cast of Mind*, B. Ingrid Olson's yearlong exhibition at i8 Grandi at the Marshall House in Reykjavík, Iceland (January 20–December 20, 2023).

Published in 2026 by Dancing Foxes Press, Brooklyn, New York

ISBN: 978-1-954947-20-7

Edited by Lucy Flint and B. Ingrid Olson
Proofreading by Polly Watson
Design by Chad Kloepfer

Printed and bound by Tallinn Printing, Estonia

Library of Congress Control Number: 2025949082

Dancing Foxes Press
16 Lefferts Place
Brooklyn, New York 11238
dfpress.org

Distributed by
ARTBOOK | D.A.P.
75 Broad Street, Suite 630
New York, New York 10004
artbook.com

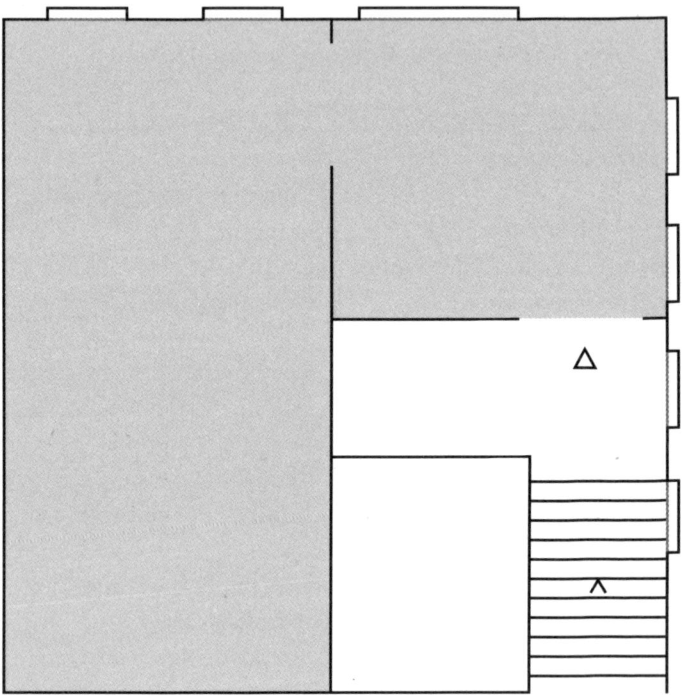

i8 Grandi
The Marshall House
Grandagarður 20, 101
Reykjavík, Iceland